THE COMPLETE
HSA GUIDEBOOK

How to make Health Savings Accounts work for you

FIFTEENTH EDITION

Includes healthcare reform and tax change updates

Stephen D. Neeleman, M.D.

No part of this book may be reproduced in any manner whatsoever without written permission except in the case of brief quotations embodied in critical articles and reviews. For information, address HealthEquity, 15 West Scenic Pointe Dr, Ste. 100, Draper, UT 84020, 801-727-1000.

ISBN: 978-0-692-95308-2 Printed in the United States of America.

FOREWORD

We began writing the first edition of The Complete HSA Guidebook a few months after new legislation allowed the creation of the first Health Savings Accounts (HSAs) on January 1, 2004. In the 17 years since then, people have developed an understanding of and appreciation for this important consumer-directed health benefit. Millions of Americans now use HSAs, not only to pay for immediate healthcare needs with tax-free dollars, but also to save for healthcare expenses in retirement. According to the Devenir 2020 Year-End HSA Market Statistics & Trends, there are more than 30 million HSAs, covering 63 million people, holding over $80 billion in funds.

I founded HealthEquity in 2002 with a simple mission: to "connect health and wealth." As this edition goes to print, HealthEquity members have saved more than $14 billion dollars in their HSAs. Our team of more than 3,000 HSA enthusiasts is committed to helping more and more Americans understand and use HSAs to protect themselves against unexpected healthcare expenses.

We intend to make HSAs more common than 401(k)s, because of their tax savings and their potential to lower overall healthcare expenditures for both consumers and businesses.

HealthEquity focuses on helping employers and employees manage out-of-pocket healthcare costs, which continue to increase every year. We believe that HSAs remain the best way to make excellent healthcare coverage available to businesses and consumers, to save taxes, and to reduce healthcare premium costs. We will continue to work with businesses and legislative leaders to increase access to HSAs so that every American can effectively manage their out-of-pocket health costs.

As our company grows, I stand amazed at the passion and commitment with which our teammates build relationships with and provide remarkable service for our members, clients, and partners. As a result of their skill and expertise, we are now one of the largest non-bank custodians of HSA funds in the United States.

In 2019, HealthEquity purchased WageWorks, a leading provider of consumer-directed spending accounts, including FSAs, HRAs, commuter accounts, and COBRA services. This acquisition strengthened HealthEquity, enhancing our ability to meet our clients' needs by expanding our range of products and continuing our commitment to help Americans manage out-of-pocket expenses for healthcare, dependent day care, and commuting expenses.

In 2021, HealthEquity purchased Luum, best known for its powerful Commute platform. Commute goes beyond merely managing complex mobility and parking programs; it does so in a way that also reduces drive-alone rates, which protects the environment and promotes employee health and flexibility.

On behalf of our entire team, I hope this publication helps you understand HSAs and encourages you to consider investing in one.

Sincerely,

Stephen D. Neeleman, M.D. HealthEquity Founder and Vice Chairman

Salt Lake City, Utah
October 2021

TABLE OF CONTENTS

CHAPTER 1

Introduction

Health Savings Accounts benefit individuals.

Because Health Savings Accounts (HSAs) provide more tax advantages than any other savings vehicle in the United States today, you should learn how to become eligible to open one so you can start reducing your tax burden, increasing your retirement savings, and protecting yourself against rising medical costs.

Like other retirement savings plans, HSAs allow you to roll over unused funds every year for future use, transfer the account to your spouse upon death, or distribute the funds to your heirs…but HSAs provide additional important advantages over other retirement accounts.

If you contribute to an IRA or 401(k), you don't pay tax on your contributions or account earnings, but you do pay tax when you withdraw the funds during retirement. Though you don't pay tax on distributions from a Roth IRA, you do pay tax on the money you contribute.

If you use a Health Flexible Spending Account (FSA), you contribute and spend tax-free dollars, but will lose any funds you have not spent at the end of the year.

Only HSAs provide what is known as a triple tax advantage: you make tax-deductible contributions, your account grows and earns interest free of federal (and most state) income tax, and your distributions (when used for qualified medical expenses) are also free of these taxes. You also have the flexibility to invest your HSA funds which, while riskier, increases your potential for growth.

Because of these significant tax savings, the IRS restricts ownership of HSAs somewhat. Only individuals covered by a high-deductible health plan (HDHP) may open an HSA. An HSA-qualified HDHP must meet government-mandated limits on minimum deductibles and maximum out-of-pocket expenses. These requirements, along with contribution limits, change slightly from year to year.

Several other restrictions exist:

- You may have no other health coverage (except certain permitted coverage).

- You may not be enrolled in Medicare.

- You may not be claimed as a dependent on someone else's tax return.

HSAs provide significant tax benefits, and solve several important insurance-related problems: by design, they directly reward wellness, provide more choice and flexibility than traditional healthcare, and help individuals manage chronic illness by encouraging the development of more knowledgeable and engaged healthcare consumers.

Heath Savings Accounts benefit employers.

HDHPs and HSAs provide a means of controlling soaring healthcare costs in a way that does not impair employees' access to quality healthcare. Besides saving money on overall reductions in premium costs, employers also pay fewer taxes because contributions to their employees' HSAs are tax deductible.

Health Savings Accounts benefit healthcare.

Because an HSA-qualified HDHP provides financial incentives to manage healthcare expenses and increase influence over healthcare decisions, participants are encouraged to become careful healthcare consumers who demand and receive better value for their healthcare dollars—increasing accountability, competitive pricing, and responsible consumption.

This publication is organized into three sections so you can easily find the information you need.

Section 1 explains foundational terms and concepts. It also describes HSAs in depth and then steps back to provide context as to how HSAs compare to and interact with other consumer-driven healthcare products.

Section 2 provides an owner's manual for HSAs: everything you need to know to wisely use this important savings vehicle to meet your present and future financial and healthcare needs—all presented in an easy-to-read, sequential format. Topics include:

- Opening an HSA

- Contributing to an HSA

- Using HSA funds

- Saving and investing HSA funds

Section 3 helps you set up a record keeping system, explains the paperwork you will receive, and provides information for employers who are considering making HSAs available to their employees.

Choosing an HDHP/HSA combination may require you to make some changes in the way you think about and use healthcare, but you do not need to compromise the quality of the healthcare you receive. By strategically contributing to your HSA and your other retirement accounts, you can reduce your tax burden and increase financial stability in your retirement years, because according to the Employee Benefit Research Institute (EBRI), a married couple will need approximately $270,000 on average to pay for their medical needs in retirement.[1]

Employees of all ages should start taking advantage of this retirement strategy. It's never too early or too late to save for retirement. If you are young and just starting out in your career, thinking of your HSA as a type of retirement vehicle and contributing with that mindset means that you have the potential to save hundreds of thousands of dollars in your HSA to help meet your financial objectives when you retire.

If you will retire soon and have recently discovered the usefulness of an HSA as an additional retirement account, you still have time to take advantage of the many benefits of an HSA.

---

1   https://www.ebri.org/docs/default-source/ebri-press-release/pr-1264-savingstargets-28may20.pdf?sfvrsn=5e993d2f_2

Summary

- HSAs provide a triple-tax benefit: pre-tax contributions, tax-free account growth, and tax-free distributions, if used for qualified medical expenses. Other health savings and retirement savings offer only one or two of the three tax advantages.

- HSAs solve several important insurance-related problems: they reward wellness, allow for tax-free funds to pay out-of-pocket medical expenses, provide more choice and flexibility than traditional healthcare, protect from post-retirement medical expenses, and help manage chronic illness, creating more knowledgeable and engaged healthcare consumers.

- HSAs also benefit employers by reducing their tax burden (because employer contributions to employees' HSA are tax deductible).

- HSAs benefit healthcare in general by increasing consumer awareness—especially through comparison shopping and research.

CHAPTER 2
Definitions and Explanations

Chapter overview

This chapter defines and explains foundational concepts used throughout the rest of the publication. Mark this chapter so you can refer back to it as you read.

The following terms and concepts will help you understand the unique benefits of Health Savings Accounts (HSAs) and compare the features of various types of health plans.

Remember that to open and contribute to an HSA, you must meet the following Internal Revenue Service (IRS) requirements:

- You must be covered under an HSA-qualified high-deductible health plan (HDHP) on the first day of the month in which you open an HSA or make a contribution to an HSA.[1]

- You may have no other health coverage, unless permitted under IRS guidelines.[2]

- You cannot be enrolled in Medicare.[3]

- You cannot be claimed as a dependent on someone else's tax return.[4]

Although you must be an eligible individual to open or contribute to an HSA, you do not have to be covered under an HDHP to maintain the account, earn tax-free interest and investment dividends, or distribute money from the account for qualified medical expenses. You get to keep, grow, and spend all of the money in the account even if you leave your employer or lose your qualifying HDHP coverage.[5]

Health coverage terms

Deductibles

HealthCare.gov defines a deductible as the amount of covered expenses that you must pay before your health coverage company (which may be an insurance company or a third-party administrator) starts paying covered medical claims, with the exception of preventive care. (See the section on "First-dollar coverage" later in this chapter.) This deductible typically resets or starts over every plan year.

The plan year may align with the calendar year (January 1 to December 31), or refer to some other 12-month period that your employer or insurer chooses. Some plans even allow deductibles to accumulate for more than 12 months. (See the "Carry-over deductible" section later in this chapter.)

1 IRC §223(c)(1)(A)(i)
2 IRC §223(c)(1)(A)(ii)
3 IRC §223(b)(7)
4 IRC §223(b)(6)
5 IRS Notice 2004-2 Q&A 20

In order to qualify as an HSA-qualified HDHP, an HDHP must adhere to limits for both minimum deductible and maximum out-of-pocket expenses. These limits may change year to year because of increases in the consumer price index (CPI). The IRS typically announces changes in May or June before the change takes effect.[6]

2021	Single	Family
Minimum annual deductible	$1,400	$2,800
Out-of-pocket maximum	$7,000	$14,000
2022	Single	Family
Minimum annual deductible	$1,400	$2,800
Out-of-pocket maximum	$7,050	$14,100

Embedded deductible

Some HDHPs provide multiple deductibles or embedded deductibles. In such plans, the lowest deductible determines if the HDHP qualifies for an HSA.[7] If you meet the individual deductible for one family member under plans that qualify, you are not required to meet the higher annual deductible for the family.

If either the deductible for the entire family or the deductible for an individual family member is less than the minimum annual deductible for family coverage allowed by the IRS, then the plan is not considered an HSA-qualified HDHP.

Examples: Embedded deductible

Elliott has family health insurance coverage for 2021, with an annual deductible of $3,500 and an individual deductible (or embedded deductible) of $1,500 for each family member.

---

6   Rev. Proc. 2020-32
7   IRS Notice 2004-50 Q&A 20

The plan does not qualify as an HSA-qualified HDHP, because the deductible for an individual family member is below the minimum annual deductible of $2,800 for family coverage in 2021.[8]

Sheela's family health insurance coverage for 2021 has an annual deductible of $6,000 and an individual deductible (or embedded deductible) of $3,000 for each family member.

Sheela's plan qualifies as an HSA-qualified HDHP, because the deductible for an individual family member is above the minimum annual deductible of $2,800 for family coverage in 2021.[9]

Carry-over deductible

Some health plans allow expenses that were applied to the previous deductible to be applied, or carried over, to the new policy when the plan year resets. Usually, the carry-over deductible is applied for expenses incurred at the end of the plan year during a certain period of time (usually three months before the plan year ends.)[10]

This is not a requirement, but it is an added benefit when expenses occur late in the year. In some circumstances, this type of carry-over deductible will cause your HDHP to lose HSA eligibility. Because the deductible includes more than 12 months, recalculate the IRS minimum deductible limit to see what deductible limits would be required for your plan to remain HSA qualified.

$$(\text{\# months in plan} \div 12) \times \text{annual deductible}$$

Example: Carry-over deductible

Matt has a plan that allows him to include expenses from 15 months (a three-month carry-over) to satisfy the deductible.

- Individual policy minimum deductible for 2021: **15/12 x $1,400 = $1,750**

- Family policy minimum deductible for 2021: **15/12 x $2,800 = $3,500**

---

8   IRS Notice 2004-2 Q&A 3
9   IRS Notice 2004-2 Q&A 3
10   IRS Notice 2004-50 Q&A 24

Instead of the limits listed in the previous table, Matt's HDHP must satisfy these higher amounts to qualify for an HSA.

Copayments vs. coinsurance

A copayment is a fixed-dollar payment a patient makes per doctor visit, treatment, test, prescription, etc. For example, you might pay $35 for each office visit and $50 for an x-ray.

Coinsurance is the percentage of a medical expense for which the patient is responsible. For example, after you meet your deductible, you might pay 20% of your medical expenses until you reach your out-of-pocket maximum for the year.

Out-of-pocket maximum

The out-of-pocket maximum is the upper limit of your financial exposure during a plan year. In some HDHPs, the out-of-pocket maximum and the deductible are the same amount.

With HDHPs, the amounts you pay for in-network deductibles, copayments, or coinsurance (but not insurance premiums) are included toward your out-of-pocket maximum.[11] Whether out-of-network charges are included in your out-of-pocket maximum can vary by plan.

Once you reach your plan's limit for the year, your health coverage pays all additional in-network, eligible expenses, regardless of the plan's usual copayment or coinsurance arrangements. Some plans refer to this maximum out-of-pocket limit as the stop-loss limit.

Remember, the maximum out-of-pocket expense limit often applies only to in-network care. Health plans may require higher out-of-pocket limits for out-of-network care. For more information, see the "Networks and discounts" section later in this chapter. If a plan has separate out-of-pocket maximums for each family member, the sum of these limits must be equal to, or less than $14,000 in 2021.

---

11   IRS Notice 2004-50 Q&A 21

Example: Out-of-pocket maximum

Tricia has a deductible of $1,500 and an out-of-pocket maximum of $3,000.

Tricia pays up to her $1,500 deductible, after which her plan agrees to split the bill 80/20. The plan pays 80% of covered medical expenses after the deductible, and Tricia pays 20% in coinsurance.

If Tricia has additional eligible expenses after she reaches her deductible, she pays 20% of those bills until she spends another $1,500 out of her own pocket. These limits may not apply to out-of-network or ineligible expenses.

When her total spending for eligible expenses reaches $3,000, her out-of-pocket maximum, her health plan pays 100% of the rest of her covered medical expenses for that plan year.

Example: Multiple out-of-pocket maximum limits[12]

Dean, Laurie, and their two children have a family plan. Their plan specifies that each family member's in-network, out-of-pocket maximum is $3,000 (and $12,000 for the entire family), after which the plan pays 100%.

Because the 2021 HDHP out-of-pocket maximum per family is $14,000, their plan qualifies them to make HSA contributions.

$$4 \times \$3,000 = \$12,000$$

$$\$12,000 < \$14,000$$

However, if they had three children, their plan would not qualify because the maximum out-of-pocket limit would be higher than the legal maximum.

$$5 \times \$3,000 = \$15,000$$

$$\$15,000 > \$14,000$$

---

12   IRS Notice 2004-50 Q&A 20, Example 1

Yearly or lifetime benefit limits

The Patient Protection and Affordable Care Act (PPACA) prohibits insurers from imposing lifetime limits on benefits. Before healthcare reform, if you exceeded your plan's yearly or lifetime benefit limits for a medical condition, you had to use your HSA or other funds to make up the difference. This provision, which became effective September 23, 2010, affects all existing insurance plans.

Preventive care

First-dollar coverage

Your insurance company may cover some of your medical costs, especially for preventive care and some chronic conditions, at no cost to you and before you meet your deductible (referred to as "first-dollar coverage").

Beginning September 23, 2010, the PPACA requires all new group health plans and plans in the individual market to provide first-dollar coverage for preventive services, including immunizations, preventive care for infants, children, and adolescents, and preventive care and screenings for women.

On July 17, 2019, the IRS and Health and Human Services expanded the list of preventive services that health plans may select for first-dollar coverage without jeopardizing the HSA eligibility of an HDHP.[13] This expanded list includes treatments for conditions such as congestive heart failure, asthma, diabetes, and depression.[14]

The definition of preventive care that applies to HSA-qualified HDHPs generally excludes any service or benefit intended to treat an existing illness, injury, or condition. However, in some situations, treatment beyond strictly preventive care screening is allowed.

Employers and health plans will have flexibility to incorporate items from this list into their plan designs, so check with your plan administrator to find out what is included. Preventive care includes, but is not limited to, the following:[15]

- Periodic health evaluations, including tests and diagnostic procedures ordered in connection with routine examinations, such as annual physicals

---

13   www.irs.gov/newsroom/irs-expands-list-of-preventive-care-for-hsa-participants-to-include-certain-care-for-chronic-conditions
14   IRS Notice 2019-45
15   IRS Notices 2004-23 and 2019-45

- Routine prenatal and well-child care

- Child and adult immunizations

- Tobacco cessation programs

- Obesity weight-loss programs

- Some medications which are intended to prevent disease (such as blood pressure and cholesterol medications)

- Screening services, including screening services for the following:

  - Cancer

  - Heart and vascular diseases

  - Infectious diseases

  - Mental health conditions

  - Substance abuse

  - Metabolic, nutritional, and endocrine conditions

  - Musculoskeletal disorders

  - Obstetric and gynecological conditions

  - Pediatric conditions

  - Vision and hearing disorders

Network considerations

If your health plan has negotiated rates with a specific network of providers, be aware that only first-dollar preventive services provided through an in-network provider must be covered at no cost sharing and before the deductible is satisfied. Your health plan may allow you to receive these services from an out-of-network provider, but you may have to pay for the services.

Networks and discounts

In general, the combination of an HSA and HDHP provides the most flexible type of healthcare arrangement available. The money in the HSA is yours to spend and save, which means you can use it to obtain treatment from virtually any licensed healthcare provider, whether in or out of your health plan's network.

In-network providers

Because a plan negotiates lower prices for services received "in-network," your HSA money goes further if you use facilities and see providers within your health plan's network. Healthcare providers—doctors, hospitals, and other healthcare facilities—participating in your plan's network have agreed to provide members of your plan a discount on their usual charges.

Not only will you generally pay less money if you use your HSA only for services covered under your plan and consult only providers who participate in your plan's network, but all of your HSA expenditures will count toward your deductible and toward your plan's out-of-pocket limits.

Repricing

If your HDHP distinguishes between in- and out-of-network providers, the insurer will modify ("reprice") your healthcare costs when you use in-network providers. Repricing refers to the adjustment of healthcare providers' prices to reflect discounts your health plan may have negotiated with the provider. Qualified HDHPs are not required to use networks with whom they have negotiated discounts but they often do, providing significant cost savings to their members. You may also see repricing for out-of-network providers, but these discounts are usually less than those provided for in-network care.

Example: Paying a network provider

Hope's doctor charges $150 for a visit for an acute sore throat.

As a provider in her health plan's network, her doctor has agreed to accept $75 from her plan for this type of visit.

Hope does not pay her provider the $150 charge at the time of the visit. Instead, because her provider is in her plan's network, she waits for the health plan to reprice the claim, applying the discount that her provider agreed to accept. She may also receive a bill directly from her doctor for the adjusted amount.

If she has not yet met her deductible at the time of the visit, she pays the $75 out of her HSA (or from another account, with post-tax dollars). This amount is also credited toward her plan's annual out-of-pocket limit (the limit on how much she can expect to spend in a given year before the plan takes over entirely).

Usual, customary, and reasonable amounts

Plans typically pay only what they consider usual, customary, and reasonable (UCR)— the estimated "going rate" paid in your geographical area for a given medical service or procedure. Any expenses above that amount that are not paid by an HDHP are not required to apply toward your deductible or to be included in determining your maximum out-of-pocket expenses.[16]

Example: Fee charged by an out-of-network provider

Your plan determines that the reasonable cost of a certain type of surgery is $2,000, a price it has negotiated with its in-network providers. You go to an out-of-network provider who charges $2,500. Your insurance will pay only $2,000 of this bill, and the additional $500 you pay may or may not apply to your health plan's deductible or out-of-pocket limit.

Inquire as to whether your HDHP has separate limits for in- and out-of-network providers and whether its network includes the providers you want to use for medical care. You can get this information from your employer's benefits administrator, your health plan, your HR team, or the summary of benefits and coverage (SBC) given to you during open enrollment.

Refusal of charges

If your provider has not contracted with your plan, then the plan is not obligated to accept the provider's full charges and you may still need to pay the bill.

---

16   IRS Notice 2004-50 Q&A 16

Example: UCRs and deductibles

Naomi's doctor charges $150 for an x-ray. Her insurance company decides that the usual and customary charge is $130 and then pays half of this reduced amount, based on a 50% coinsurance provision for x-rays in Naomi's plan.

Naomi pays the remaining half, and possibly the $20 difference between the UCR and the billed charge if the doctor does not have a negotiated discount agreement.

If she has to pay the extra $20, the visit costs Naomi $85. The doctor still receives her usual fee of $150: $85 from Naomi and $65 from her insurance company. However, because her health plan has not allowed the full amount of her doctor's charges to be considered, the extra $20 does not count toward Naomi's deductible and out-of-pocket limit for the year.

Referrals and authorization

Even if you use network providers, you may still need to obtain a referral from your primary care provider to see a specialist or seek authorization for a medical procedure from your health plan.

Gatekeepers

Depending on your plan's rules, you may also need to use a gatekeeper or primary care physician to obtain referrals and authorizations for certain medical services or procedures. Certain primary care providers, such as General Practitioners (GPs), family practitioners, pediatricians, and internists generally act as gatekeepers, overseeing and coordinating all aspects of a patient's care.

Referrals

Many managed care plans require a referral from your primary care provider in order for you to see a specialist. Even if your provider allows you to make an appointment with a specialist directly, your insurance might not cover the visit if you did not first receive a referral, so familiarize yourself with your health plan's guidelines to avoid unexpected expenses.

Authorization

In addition to a referral, you may also need authorization—your health plan's permission to proceed with a medical or surgical procedure. Without authorization, the plan may refuse to pay for the procedure, even if the procedure might otherwise have been covered.

If you fail to obtain a referral or authorization when one is required, your plan may charge you a higher copayment, coinsurance rate, or even a flat-dollar penalty. The excess copayments, coinsurance, and penalties may not count toward your HDHP's out-of-pocket limit for the year; however, you may pay these expenses out of your HSA.

Failure to understand and follow your plan's rules can cost you money.

Summary

- In order to be HSA-qualified, your HDHP must meet standards set by the government for minimum deductible and maximum out-of-pocket expenses.

- A deductible is the amount of covered expenses that you must pay for in a given plan year before your insurance company starts paying covered medical claims.

- Copayments are a set dollar amount charged for services such as office visits and tests. Co-insurance is a percentage of the overall bill that you are responsible for, after you meet your deductible.

- You generally save money by receiving treatment from in-network providers and in-network facilities, which have negotiated discounts with your insurance company.

CHAPTER 3
Health Savings Accounts

Chapter overview

A Health Savings Account, referred to as an HSA throughout, is a tax-advantaged savings account that you own.

An HSA is a tax-exempt trust or custodial account that you set up with a qualified HSA trustee (which could be a bank, insurance company, or Treasury-approved non-bank custodian or trustee) to pay or reimburse certain qualified medical expenses you incur. Many HSA administrators provide online banking services similar to those of a personal bank account. In most cases, the cash balance is federally insured, but read the literature from your custodian or trustee to see if your account is federally insured. HSA holders may wish to increase their earning potential by investing in qualified investment accounts such as stocks, mutual funds, and other investments (which are not federally insured).[1]

The HDHP protects you from major medical costs, such as catastrophic illness, prolonged hospitalization, and other large medical bills.

If you qualify,[2] you and your employer can make tax-deductible contributions to your HSA and you can use the funds, tax-free (in most situations), to cover various qualified medical expenses.

If you contribute more than you spend from your HSA, those funds accumulate and increase in value over the years—especially if you choose to invest money from your HSA. Americans have the opportunity to prepare for both their future healthcare and retirement needs by thoughtfully using their HSA alongside their 401(k) and other retirement accounts.

For information about who can open or contribute to an HSA, see Chapters 5 and 6.

For information about saving and investing HSA funds, see Chapter 8.

---

1 Investments made available to HSA holders are subject to risk, including the possible loss of the principal invested, and are not FDIC or NCUA insured, or guaranteed.
2 You must be covered under an HSA-qualified HDHP, you may have no other health coverage (with some exceptions), and you can neither be enrolled in Medicare nor claimed as a dependent on someone else's tax return.

What is an HSA?

All health plans—whether they are PPOs, HMOs, or even HDHPs—typically provide "use it or lose it" funds. If you pay more for your share of the cost of coverage (remember that if you're employed, your employer probably pays a significant portion of the cost) than your health plan needs to cover your medical expenses, you do not benefit financially because there's no refund of unused premium payments.

Because an HSA-qualified high-deductible health plan (HDHP) generally has lower premiums than a traditional plan, you can contribute the difference to your HSA to save for future healthcare expenses. In addition, you save money on taxes with your HSA contributions and have more flexibility and control when spending or saving HSA funds. Because you own your HSA, you keep the savings when you spend less than you contribute in any given year.

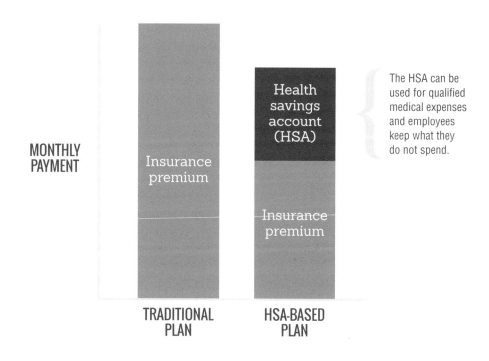

MONTHLY PAYMENT

Insurance premium

Health savings account (HSA)

Insurance premium

The HSA can be used for qualified medical expenses and employees keep what they do not spend.

TRADITIONAL PLAN

HSA-BASED PLAN

You and your employer can make tax-deductible contributions to your HSA as long as you are enrolled in a qualified HDHP and have no disqualifying healthcare coverage. Review the previous chapter for HSA-qualified HDHP requirements.

Your HSA can be used, tax-free, to cover the following expenses:

- Your insurance or coverage deductible,

- Copayments and coinsurance until you reach your health plan's out-of-pocket maximum (the HDHP covers the rest),

- Qualified prescription, medical, vision, or dental expenses, and

- Other qualified healthcare expenses that insurance plans might exclude.

Tax advantage

An HSA provides triple-tax savings because you pay no taxes on your contributions, earnings, or distributions—if you follow the rules. The three tax advantages are:

- Contributions to the HSA are tax-deductible for you—whether they come from you, your employer, or from family and friends.[3] As an added benefit, unlike a 401(k), the money you and your employer contribute to your HSA through payroll is not subject to Social Security (FICA) and Medicare taxes.[4] Contributions are tax-deductible in most states as well, with just a few exceptions. Contact your tax advisor for specific states that may not exempt HSA contributions from taxation.

- Your account and investment earnings grow tax-free.[5]

- Any amount paid or distributed from your HSA is tax-free, as long as you use it for qualified medical expenses.[6]

Contributing funds to your HSA on a pre-tax basis not only reduces your income tax liability, but it may also reduce other employment-related taxes, including the following:

- **Federal Insurance Contributions Act (FICA)**. Your employer withholds FICA taxes from each paycheck you receive. FICA taxes include a 6.2% Social Security tax, a 1.45% Medicare tax and a 0.9% Medicare surtax for those earning more than

---

3   IRC §223(a), IRS Notice 2004-2 Q&A 11
4   IRC §106(d)(1), IRS Notice 2004-2 Q&A 19
5   IRS Notice 2004-2 Q&A 20
6   IRC §223(f)(1)

$200,000. Your employer also pays a 6.2% Social Security tax and a 1.45% Medicare tax based on your earnings.

By contributing to your HSA using pre-tax payroll deductions (rather than rolling over funds or accepting contributions from others), you not only reduce your taxable income, but you also reduce the amount you and your employer pay in FICA tax.

- **Federal Unemployment Tax Act (FUTA)**. Your employer pays FUTA taxes based on your wages: 6.2% on the first $7,000 you earn. This amount is not withheld from your wages.

When you or your employer contribute to your HSA, it lowers the earnings used when calculating the employer-paid FUTA tax.

- **State Unemployment Tax ACT (SUTA)**. SUTA is the state version of FUTA. Each state sets its own unemployment tax rate and wage base.

When you or your employer contribute to your HSA pre-tax, it lowers the earnings used to calculate the employer-paid SUTA tax in most states.

Ownership

All of the money in your HSA is yours (including contributions from your employer) and remains yours even if you leave your job, lose your qualifying health plan, or retire.

In other words, you cannot lose your HSA funds. It is not a "use-it-or-lose-it" type of account.[7] For this reason, many people use their HSA as an additional savings and investment account for healthcare expenses in retirement.

Because of the unique tax advantages, the government limits the amount of money you can contribute each year to your HSA. If you contribute too much, you will pay income tax on the additional amount, as well as a penalty. For more information about HSA contributions, see Chapter 6.

---

7   IRC §223(d)(1)(E)

HSA contribution limit	2021	2022
Individual	$3,600	$3,650
Family	$7,200	$7,300
Additional catch-up contribution for those 55 and older	$1,000	$1,000

As your balance rolls over from year to year, it earns interest. When your balance is large enough, you may be able to invest it, tax-free, the same way you invest dollars from other retirement accounts. Check with your custodian about investment vehicles and minimum requirements. For more information about saving and investing HSA funds, see Chapter 8.

Choice and flexibility

An HSA-qualified HDHP gives you greater choice and flexibility when managing your healthcare options. You alone decide how to use the money in your HSA, including whether to save it or spend it for healthcare expenses.

Pay for qualified medical expenses

Your HSA can be used to reimburse any out-of-pocket healthcare expenses that are not covered by your health plan, or those expenses that you could otherwise deduct on your federal tax returns. In general, the funds in your HSA can be used to pay for more expenses than your health plan typically covers.

IRS Publications 502 and 969, when used together, provide guidance about qualified expenses.[8]

Cover work/life transitions

You can use an HSA to bridge events such as unemployment, job changes, and periods of disability by paying for health plan premiums or healthcare directly.[9] Your HSA can be used to pay Consolidated Omnibus Budget Reconciliation Act (COBRA) premiums (for continued healthcare coverage through your former employer)[10] or premiums for long-term care.

---

8   IRC §223(d)(2)(A). IRC §213(d). IRS Notice 2004-2 Q&A 26. IRS Publication 502
9   IRC §223(d)(2)(c)(iii), IRS Notice 2004-2 Q&A 27
10   IRC §223(d)(2)(C)(ii), IRS Notice 2004-2 Q&A 27

Pay for post-retirement healthcare expenses

HSAs help you save for health expenses you will incur in retirement, tax free. You can use your HSA to pay for out-of-pocket expenses including deductibles, copays and coinsurance, and Medicare premiums (except Medigap) including the following:[11]

- Part A (hospital and inpatient services)

- Part B (physician and outpatient services)

- Part C (Medicare Advantage plans)

- Part D (prescription drugs)

Manage the variability of expenses

HSAs provide a way to manage the variability of healthcare expenses. For example, one year you may have just a few healthcare expenses, while the next year you may meet your deductible mid-year and still have more expenses. Because an HSA allows you discretion in when you reimburse yourself, you can choose to save your money for times when you have more expenses. HSAs can only be used for expenses incurred after you establish your HSA.[12]

Benefit from a healthy lifestyle

Since 2011, HSA-qualified HDHPs are required to cover 100% of standard preventive care services,[13] as designated by your health plan. If you take advantage of preventive care services and adopt healthy lifestyle habits, you may reduce your medical expenses, potentially increasing your ability to pay for healthcare costs in retirement.

How do HSAs compare to IRAs or 401(k) plans?

HSAs have features in common with retirement accounts such as tax-advantaged individual retirement accounts (IRAs) and 401(k) plans. Like IRAs and 401(k) plans, HSAs allow year-to-year rollover, portability, choice of account investments, and survivor benefits.

---

11 IRC §223(d)(2)(C)(iv); IRS Notice 2004-2 Q&A 27
12 IRS Notice 2004-50 Q&A 39
13 The PPACA added PHS Act §2713

These investment opportunities as well as others (such as Roth IRAs, 529 education accounts, and Coverdell accounts) have helped consumers save for retirement and other expenses using tax-free funds.

How an HSA is like a 401(k) or an IRA

- You and your employer can both make pre-tax contributions to your account.

- Your unused contributions carry over from year to year.

- Your funds grow tax free for as long as you own the account.

- Your account can be inherited by your survivors. (Your spouse can inherit your account as his or her own HSA, tax-free.) [14]

How an HSA is better

- Neither you nor your employer pay FICA taxes (Social Security and Medicare) on HSA contributions made through payroll.[15]

- You can contribute money from both earned and unearned income up to the IRS annual limit, as long as you have HSA-qualified HDHP coverage and do not have any disqualifying coverage. Family members and other individuals can contribute to your account as well, but only you and your employer receive the tax benefits.[16] Note that your tax benefits are limited to the amount of your taxable income and you cannot carry your deduction forward to another year.[17]

- You can use HSA funds to pay qualified medical expenses incurred by your spouse and your IRS-qualified dependents—all tax-free.

- If you are no longer employed, you can still make tax-advantaged contributions to your HSA if you are still covered by an HSA-qualified HDHP and are not enrolled in Medicare or have any other disqualifying coverage.

- If you use the funds for qualified medical expenses, you can make tax-free distributions at any time without tax or penalty.[18]

---

14 IRC §223(f)(B)(A)
15 IRS Notice 2004-2 Q&A 19
16 IRS Notice 2004-2 Q&A 18
17 IRS Notice 2004-2 Q&A 17
18 IRC §223(f)(1), IRS Notice 2004-2 Q&A 25 & 26

- After age 65, you can use HSA distributions on anything you wish, without paying a 20% penalty. However, such distributions will be subject to income taxation if not used for qualified medical expenses.

Is an HSA right for you?

An HSA allows you peace of mind in having resources set aside for healthcare expenses, both the expected and unexpected ones. It also encourages you to be more involved with decisions on how to spend healthcare dollars and helps you to budget effectively. To make the best use of your account, regularly assess your financial situation and consider the type of healthcare you have used in the past and expect to use in the future.

Consider if you are eligible to establish and contribute to an HSA, have benefits paid from an HSA, or (if you aren't able to contribute on a pre-tax basis through your employer) whether you can claim the tax deduction for a contribution. Whether an HDHP/HSA combination is right for you depends on a number of factors, including the health needs of you and your family, and how often you expect to change jobs or health plans. For specific side-by-side cost comparison scenarios, see the "Examples" section of Chapter 8.

Tax-free retirement spending

Even with the passage of the PPACA and changes in Medicare, healthcare costs will continue to rise significantly, especially in retirement. Industry analysts warn that many retirees will fall short of the amounts needed to cover the gaps in medical coverage as they age. The Employee Benefit Research Institute (EBRI) estimates that an average 65-year-old couple needs $270,000 in savings to cover medical costs in retirement (premiums for Medicare Parts B, D, and perhaps Medigap Plan G, deductibles, and out-of-pocket spending for outpatient prescription drugs). A couple with higher prescription drug expenses will need about $325,000.[19]

Without an HSA, many retirees pay for their share of medical expenses by taking distributions from their 401(k)s and other retirement savings plans. Unfortunately, these distributions are taxable.[20]

19 https://www.ebri.org/docs/default-source/ebri-issue-brief/ebri_ib_506_savingstargets-28may20.pdf
20 IRC §402(a)

By using accumulated balances in an HSA, a retiree can save significant amounts of money on taxes by paying for qualified medical expenses with tax-free dollars.

As an added benefit, at age 65 you can spend your HSA funds for any purpose you wish. If the funds are used to pay for qualified medical expenses, you won't pay taxes on distributions; if the money is used to pay for anything other than a qualified medical expense, you will have to pay income taxes on the distribution, but you won't have to pay a penalty. Because of this, an HSA used with an IRA or 401(k)/403(b) can make your retirement savings go much further than they would without an HSA.

Chronic conditions

When you have a choice of health plans, whether from a selection of plans offered by your employer or as an individual purchaser, consider how you have used healthcare in the past.

A chronic condition—one that lasts a long time or recurs frequently and can be treated but not cured—generally requires substantial healthcare on an ongoing basis. An HSA may benefit you or a family member who suffers from a chronic disease such as diabetes, heart dysfunction, or asthma because some HDHP policies treat medications for chronic conditions as "preventive care," covering these medications before you meet your deductible.

Not all chronic conditions are expensive to treat; however, they may require monitoring, adherence to treatment regimens, or perhaps the use of medical devices not typically provided by health plans but considered qualified medical expenses for purposes of an HSA. You can often pay for these items from your HSA.

Before committing to an HSA-qualified HDHP plan, compare the flexibility and tax advantages of HSA distributions with the coverage offered by lower-deductible and typically higher-premium traditional health plans in order to choose the best option for your particular circumstances.

As premiums, copays, and coinsurance costs all continue to increase, HSA-qualified plans have the potential to provide long-term savings.

Unanticipated expenses

Although you and your family may enjoy good health, healthcare coverage is important because you could face an unexpected or expensive medical emergency or major illness.

Determine if you can set aside money in an HSA on a regular basis to cover your usual healthcare needs, such as medications and office visits for minor illnesses or injuries.

Many people do not reach their deductibles because they do not spend much on healthcare in a typical year. An HSA-qualified health plan helps these people by allowing them to save tax-free in an account for use in years when they have more healthcare expenses.

Job changes

Consider your job, industry, and occupation, as well as your career stage and plans. People tend to change jobs more often in some fields than in others and younger people tend to move around more than people who are more established in their careers.

You can continue coverage under an HDHP when you have a COBRA-qualifying event, just like any other plan and you can use your HSA to pay COBRA premiums and healthcare expenses during a period when you lack other coverage.[21] In this way, an HSA can provide an important safety net in a difficult economy.

Legal considerations

Since the first HSA was created in 2004, various laws have shaped and defined the accounts.

On December 8, 2003, President George W. Bush signed Section 1201 of the Medicare Prescription Drug Improvement and Modernization Act of 2003, which became Public Law No. 108-173. This provision adds Section 223 to the Internal Revenue Code (IRC) to permit eligible individuals to establish HSAs beginning in tax year 2004.

---

21   IRC §223(d)(2)(C), IRS Notice 2004-2 Q&A 27

On March 23, 2010, President Obama signed the Patient Protection and Affordable Care Act (PPACA). The PPACA applies to a broad range of healthcare issues, and some of these new requirements affect HSAs.

On March 27, 2020, President Trump signed the Coronavirus Aid, Relief, and Economic Security Act (CARES Act), which allows reimbursement from an HSA for over-the-counter medications.

The following section describes the legal framework that governs HSAs.

Trusts and HSAs

The law treats HSAs as trusts, because individual account holders own them, funds accumulate year to year, and specific rules govern them. Both state and federal laws affect HSAs.

Trusts require a fiduciary relationship: a bank, corporation, or other entity acting as a trustee holds legal title and has a legal obligation to keep and use the trust for the benefit of the equitable owner.

Trustees have legal responsibility to hold property in the best interest of or for the benefit of another entity or person, by managing and investing funds. A custodian, on the other hand, maintains an account, but has no investment or management responsibilities. An HSA trustee must be a bank, insurance company, or a non-bank entity that meets specific IRS requirements.[22]

The trustee must deal with the trust property honestly, put the beneficiary's interest above its own, and closely follow the terms of the trust. Though it may have discretion over investments and day-to-day management, the trust agreement still governs these functions. The trustee holds and administers an HSA to pay for qualified medical expenses.

Opening a trust

Many state trust laws say that the act of depositing funds into the account establishes or opens the HSA. This date may affect how much can be contributed the first year, and which expenses can be paid from the account.

---

22   IRC §223(d)(1)(B)

Some states may have different rules regarding the establishment of trusts. For example, Utah amended its trust law in 2009 to allow the establishment of the HSA to coincide with the date the account holder enrolls in a federally qualified HDHP,[23] provided that date occurs before the filing deadline (without extensions) for the account owner's federal tax return.

HDHPs and preventive care

Many states have adopted insurance laws that require health plans to provide certain healthcare benefits (especially preventive care) without first having to meet the deductible. Because this requirement might jeopardize the tax status of an HSA (by paying benefits before the minimum annual deductible has been met), laws that govern HDHPs provide a safe harbor, so HSA-qualified HDHPs can waive the deductible for preventive care benefits.[24] See Chapter 2 for a list of preventive care services that HDHPs might include.

Federal law vs. state law

In some instances, a plan might conform to federal law but not meet state requirements. When state insurance laws conflict with the federal laws governing HSAs, enrollment in an HSA might be prohibited, or perhaps allowed only in special circumstances.

Some states have enacted exemptions from state mandates for plans that meet federal criteria for HSA-qualified HDHPs. State laws may also affect the tax status of HSAs. Although federal income tax does not apply to HSA contributions, growth, or distributions (for qualified medical expenses), HSA contributions may not qualify for tax breaks according to state or local income tax laws, the state component of the tax that finances unemployment benefits, or estate law. Check with your tax advisor to determine your specific tax obligations.

Healthcare reform

When President Obama signed the PPACA into law in 2010, many HSA advocates expressed concern that the new law might undermine the success of HSAs. Instead,

---

23   UT Code §75-7-401(2)
24   IRC §223(c)(2)(C)

regulations have addressed many of the ambiguous parts of the law in a way that does not appear to restrict HSAs—and might even create a more favorable environment for them.

Several of these PPACA provisions are described below, including waiving pre-existing condition exclusions, removing lifetime and annual coverage maximums, providing first-dollar coverage for preventive care, and loosening over-the-counter (OTC) medication rules.

Health insurance exchanges

Individuals can purchase health insurance through their employer, directly from an insurance company, or through a health insurance exchange. Exchanges (such as the Health Insurance Marketplace at HealthCare.gov) allow consumers to comparison shop for standardized health packages.

Most states use the federal health insurance exchange, but 14 states and the District of Columbia created their own exchanges: California, Colorado, Connecticut, Idaho, Maryland, Massachusetts, Minnesota, Nevada, New Jersey, New York, Pennsylvania, Rhode Island, Vermont, and Washington.

Whether purchased from a federal or state exchange, HSA-qualified health plans are usually among the least expensive plans available. Healthcare reform has further assisted people at all income levels to obtain affordable coverage by providing tax credits and facilitating enrollment.

Penalties

In 2014, the PPACA instituted a penalty for choosing not to purchase health insurance. The penalty has risen every year.

- 2014: $95

- 2015: $325

- 2016-2018: $695 or up to 2.5% of income, whichever is greater[25]

In addition, families paid half the amount for each uninsured child, up to a per-family cap that increased each year.

---

25   IRC §5000A

On December 19, 2017, Congress passed the Tax Cut and Jobs Act of 2017,[26] which abolished the Affordable Care Act's penalty for not having health insurance, starting with the 2019 plan year (for which you filed taxes in 2020).

The law does not eliminate the requirement that individuals have healthcare coverage—only the financial penalty for not doing so.

Essential health benefits

As of 2014, ACA-compliant health plans (purchased by individuals from insurance companies or exchanges or offered by small employers) must cover the following items and services, referred to as "essential health benefits" or EHBs:[27]

- Ambulatory patient services

- Emergency services

- Hospitalization

- Maternity and newborn care

- Mental health and substance abuse services

- Prescription drugs

- Rehabilitative and habilitative services and devices

- Laboratory services

- Preventive and wellness services and chronic disease management

- Pediatric services, including oral and vision care

EHBs must meet certain specifications:

- A cost-sharing limit for in-network, out-of-pocket maximum of $8,550/$17,000 for single/family in 2021 and $8,700/$17,400 in 2022.

---

26   §11081 of Tax Cut and Jobs Act of 2017
27   §1302 of the Affordable Care Act

- Meet 60% actuarial value (AV) requirements, meaning that the plan must pay at least 60% of the cost of care that would be covered by a plan that had no out-of-pocket cost-sharing requirement. Federal regulations confirm that employers' contributions to HSAs count toward the 60% requirement.[28]

In addition to the ACA cost-sharing limits, HSA-qualified HDHPs must follow additional IRS rules, which apply different minimum deductible and maximum out-of-pocket limits, as listed in the "Deductibles" section of Chapter 2.

Preexisting conditions

Insurers may no longer deny coverage for treatment of pre-existing health conditions; neither can they charge higher premiums because of health status, gender, or other variables. Premiums may only vary with age (no more than 3:1—for example, a 65-year-old may pay three times what a 21-year-old pays), geography, family size, and tobacco use.

Annual and lifetime limits

Elimination of annual and lifetime limits (the total benefits an insurance company will pay in a year or in a lifetime) began with some plans in 2010. By 2014, all major medical health plans (except gap or mini-med plans) eliminated annual limits, which eliminates the need to purchase supplemental coverage.

Clinical trials

As of 2014, the PPACA prohibits insurers from dropping coverage if an individual participates in a clinical trial. Not only can insurers not drop coverage, they also cannot deny coverage for routine care that they would otherwise cover if the individual were not in a clinical trial. This applies to any clinical trial that treats cancer or other life-threatening diseases.

---

28   §1302(d)(2)(B) of the Affordable Care Act, 45 CFR §156.140(c)

Summary

- A Health Savings Account (HSA) allows you to contribute pre-tax dollars to pay for healthcare costs now and in the future, provided you are enrolled in an HSA-qualified HDHP and have no other impermissible coverage. Because you own the account, funds can continue to grow year over year.

- You can either spend all of the money in your account on healthcare or save some of it—for instance, if you have fewer expenses than contributions, if you can afford to pay for healthcare out of pocket, or if you can cover your medical expenses using another vehicle.

- HSAs have contribution limits, which increase each year based on the CPI. Anyone can contribute to your HSA, but the combined contributions from all sources must not exceed the annual limit.

CHAPTER 4

Consumer-Driven Healthcare

Chapter overview

The previous chapter described HSAs and the requirement that they be coupled with an HSA-qualified HDHP. This chapter describes HDHPs within the context of consumer-driven healthcare (CDHC) and discusses the relationship of HSAs to other consumer-driven benefit (CDB) accounts.

A consumer-driven health plan (CDHP) is a comprehensive health insurance plan that combines a lower-premium, high-deductible health plan (HDHP) with a tax-preferred healthcare account—a Health Savings Account (HSA), Health Reimbursement Arrangement (HRA), or Flexible Spending Account (FSA). Members pay routine healthcare expenses directly from their HSA, FSA, or HRA, but a high-deductible health plan protects them from more costly medical expenses after they meet their annual out-of-pocket maximum.

With this type of plan, medical expenses are paid from three sources:

- First, the allotment of money provided by the employer in an HSA, FSA, or HRA pays healthcare costs.

- Once healthcare costs have used up this amount, the consumer pays for healthcare until the deductible is reached.

- Once the out-of-pocket maximum is reached, the health plan pays all further costs for the plan year.

For more than a decade, employers have offered various types of CDBs, such as HRAs, HSAs, FSAs, and state and federal Archer Medical Spending Accounts (MSAs). Consumers use these accounts to pay for medical copayments, dependent care, dental and vision expenses, and other medical expenses with tax-deductible (or pre-tax) dollars.

Each type of account offers advantages. In some situations, supplementing an HSA with a special-purpose FSA or HRA gives an employer useful options for making the HDHP option even more attractive to both employees and employers. Some employees use FSAs and HRAs to make their HSA balances go further, but those who contribute to an HSA may only use certain types of limited purpose FSAs or HRAs.

A CDHP solution controls costs and, at the same time, improves overall health and well-being because of its focus on cost transparency and consumer responsibility. According to a study conducted by McKinsey & Company,[1] CDHC patients were twice as likely as patients in traditional plans to ask about cost and three times as likely to choose a less expensive treatment option. Chronic patients were 20% more likely to follow treatment regimens carefully.

As mentioned before, HSA ownership requires health coverage that meets the statutory requirements for an HSA-qualified high-deductible health plan, a specific type of consumer-driven health plan. To learn what differentiates various types of CDHC and how they work with one another, read on.

HSA-qualified HDHP coverage

Only HDHPs that adhere to certain deductible and out-of-pocket limits qualify the member to make contributions to an HSA.

Like most plans, an HDHP generally covers 100% of qualified medical expenses once the member has reached their annual out-of-pocket maximum, which protects the member from large and unexpected healthcare expenses that would be difficult to pay for, even with an HSA.

Exactly what your plan covers depends on your employer, your health plan, and the choices you make from among the plans available to you. For example, some plans may pay for fertility treatments or bariatric (weight loss) surgery, while others do not. Even though some variation exists, all HDHPs must pay for certain preventive care services, according to PPACA regulations.

1   Consumer Direct Health Plan Report, McKinsey & Company

Because HDHPs vary, do not assume that your current plan covers the same items your last one did. Acquaint yourself with your new plan's provisions, which you can find in the summary of benefits and coverage (SBC) you receive during enrollment.

As mentioned in Chapter 2 in the context of deductibles, and in Chapter 3 in the context of HSAs, HDHPs must adhere to the following limits to be considered HSA-qualified.[2]

	Single		Family	
	2021	2022	2021	2022
Minimum annual deductible	≥$1,400	≥$1,400	≥$2,800	≥$2,800
Out-of-pocket maximum	≤$7,000	≤$7,050	≤$14,000	≤$14,100

Types of coverage

Self-only HDHP coverage

Self-only coverage covers only the individual member enrolled in the plan.

Family HDHP coverage

Family HDHP coverage covers an eligible individual plus at least one other individual— even if the additional person is not eligible to open an HSA. For example, the other person may have a self-only plan that does not allow them to contribute to an HSA.

Example: Family coverage

Nicholas and Opal are married and have one daughter. Nicholas selects coverage from his employer that covers his entire family. Opal has her own self-only policy from her employer that is not an HSA-qualified HDHP.

Nicholas can make a full family contribution to an HSA, provided he has no other disqualifying coverage.[3]

---

2   Rev. Proc. 2015-30
3   IRC §223(b)(5), IRS Notice 2008-59 Q&A 16

Employee plus one HDHP coverage

If an eligible individual and his or her dependent child are covered under an employee-plus-one HSA-qualified HDHP offered by the individual's employer, the IRS considers them to have family coverage, which means they can make a full family contribution to an HSA.[4]

Benefits and restrictions

The IRS is very specific about what kinds of insurance you can have along with an HSA-qualified HDHP. Having another policy with benefits that overlap some of the medical coverage in your HDHP can make you ineligible to contribute to an HSA.

This section describes some benefits that might affect HSA eligibility.

Prescription drug benefits

Some plans offer prescription drug benefits through separate plans (also called pharmacy riders) that cover prescription drugs even if the deductible has not yet been met. Such prescription drug benefits are not considered permitted coverage under HSA law, unless these riders cover only preventive care medications.[5]

An individual covered by an ineligible prescription drug plan or rider may not open or contribute to an HSA because the prescription plan provides first-dollar coverage for an ineligible benefit. See the "Preventive care" section later in this chapter for a description of first-dollar coverage.

Discount cards

Discount cards that provide price reductions on services or health products (such as prescription drugs) are allowed—so long as the member must pay the costs of the healthcare (taking into account the discount) until the deductible of the HDHP is satisfied.[6]

Hospitalization indemnity plans

An indemnity plan pays health insurance benefits in the form of cash payments rather than services, typically as a fixed amount for each day you are in the hospital. Some insurance companies call these "gap plans" or "HSA protector policies," because the

4   IRS Notice 2004-50 Q&A 12
5   IRS Notice 2004-50 Q&A 26
6   IRS Notice 2004-50 Q&A 9

plan covers you against a large bill before you meet your HDHP's deductible. This can protect your HSA dollars and help you pay hospital expenses before you build up your account balance.

Hospitalization indemnity plans require hospital admission in order for benefits to begin. They do not cover actual hospital services, such as medical tests you might have in a hospital or hospital-related facility, but only offer cash benefits for each day you are hospitalized.

Care from IHS or VA

Individuals who receive care from Indian Health Service (IHS) or the Department of Veterans Affairs (VA) (except for dental, vision, or preventive care) may be excluded from making HSA contributions for a period of time.[7] You may not make HSA contributions for a given month if you received medical benefits from VA or from an IHS facility at any time during the previous three months. However, if your spouse meets the eligibility requirements, your spouse may contribute the full family maximum and pay for the family's expenses from their Health Savings Account. Veterans are not subject to the three-month rule when receiving treatment for a service-connected disability.[8]

Other permitted coverage[9]

The tax code and the IRS have specific rules for insurance plans that are allowed to coexist with an HSA and plans that might otherwise disqualify you from owning an HSA. For a quick summary, see the following lists:

Permitted coverage

- Automobile, dental, vision, and long-term care insurance

- Coverage for a specific disease or illness, if it pays a specific dollar amount when the policy is triggered

- Indemnity plans that pay a fixed amount per day (or other period) of hospitalization

- Wellness programs offered by employers, if they do not pay significant medical benefits

7   IRS Notice 2012-14 (OJS) and 2004-50 Q&A 5 (VA)
8   IRC §223(c)(1), §4007(b) of the Surface Transportation Act of 2015 (HR 3236), IRS Notice 2015-87 Q&A 20
9   IRC §223(c)(1)(B), IRC §223(c)(3), IRS Notice 2004-50 Q&A 7–10

- Limited purpose FSAs and HRAs (limited to dental, vision, or preventive care) and post-deductible FSAs and HRAs (which pay for medical expenses after the plan deductible is met)[10]

- An employer-sponsored HRA that can only be used when you retire or after you meet your annual deductible

- Workers' compensation insurance

- Tort liability coverage

- Prescription or other discount programs

- Other health plans are permissible, even if they may not be specifically labeled as an HSA-qualified HDHP, such as the following:

  - An HSA-qualified PPO or HMO, if the deductible meets or exceeds the HDHP-required minimums and other statutory requirements

  - Family HDHP coverage with an embedded individual deductible, if the deductible is not less than the minimum required family HDHP deductible[11]

Disallowed coverage

- General FSAs or HRAs that pay for any kind of eligible medical expense before the HDHP deductible is met. (Note that limited purpose and post-deductible FSAs and HRAs are allowed.)

- A spouse's FSA or HRA, if it can pay for eligible medical expenses before the HDHP deductible is met

- Employer payments or reimbursements for medical expenses below the minimum HDHP deductible[12]

- Medicare[13]

---

10   Rev. Rul. 2004-45
11   IRS Notice 2004-50 Q&A 20
12   Rev. Rul. 2004-45
13   IRC §223(b)(7)

- Health benefits or prescription drugs received from the VA or one of its facilities in the last three months (though beginning on January 1, 2016, hospital care or medical services received under any law administered by the Secretary of Veterans Affairs for a service-connected disability is considered allowable coverage).[14,15]

- TRICARE[16]

---

14   HR 3236, IRS Notice 2004-50 Q&A 5
15   IRC §223(b)(7)
16   IRS Notice 2004-50 Q&A 6

Comparison of HSAs, FSAs, and HRAs

The following table compares three common types of medical payment accounts. Refer back to the table as you read more detailed descriptions of each account below.

	HSA	FSA	HRA
	Health Savings Account	Health Flexible Spending Account	Health Reimbursement Arrangement
Purpose	Long-term savings/ investment	Short-term spending account	Employer-funded reimbursement
Variations	Cafeteria/non-cafeteria plans	Limited purpose/ post-deductible FSA	Limited Purpose HRA | post-deductible | EBHRA | ICHRA | QSEHRA | Retiree HRA
Health plan type	HSA-qualified HDHP required	Various	Various or, in some cases, none
Account ownership	Member-owned, portable, transferrable, inheritable	Employer-owned (no portability)	Employer-owned (no portability)
Restrictions	Must have an HSA-qualified HDHP. Cannot have Medicare or other impermissible coverage. Must not be claimed as a tax dependent.	Compatible with traditional health plans	Compatible with most health plans

	HSA	FSA	HRA
Contributors	Anyone (member, employer, family member)	Member, employer	Employer only (except COBRA)
2021 contribution limits	$3,600/$7,200 (individual/family) $1,000 catch-up for over 55	Up to $2,750 (individual/family)	Varies
Employer contributions	Count towards contribution limit	Do not count towards contribution limit	N/A
Tax-deductions	Contributions, earnings, and distributions, for qualified medical expenses	Contributions and distributions, for eligible medical expenses	Contributions and distributions, for eligible medical expenses
Use-it-or-lose-it?	No	Yes	Depends on plan design
Covered individuals	Holder, spouse, other tax dependents	Employee, spouse, other tax dependents, <26-year-old children	Employee, spouse, other tax dependents, <26-year-old children

MSAs and Archer MSAs

MSAs and Archer MSAs have existed since the mid-1990s.

Promoters believed that Archer MSAs would help limit excessive use of healthcare services by making employees aware of the actual costs of medical care. Archer MSAs provided a more affordable alternative to high-priced, low-deductible health plans for small employers and self-employed individuals. Savings in the MSA could be rolled over year to year.

The fact that only self-employed individuals and employees of small businesses could enroll limited the program's impact. When MSAs were superseded by HSAs, existing MSAs were grandfathered in as HSAs. The pilot program for Archer MSAs ended December 31, 2007, and no new Archer MSAs can be opened.

FSAs[17]

An FSA allows employees to set aside pre-tax earnings to pay for benefits or expenses (such as copays, deductibles, dental, and vision expenses) that are not covered by insurance or other benefit plans.

FSAs usually offer IRS-allowed flexibility in the use-it-or-lose-it rule. Specifically, they either allow a portion of your account to carry forward to next year (up to 20% of the maximum contribution limit) or they allow a brief grace period after the year ends during which you can use the previous plan year's funds to reimburse current eligible expenses. An FSA can offer a carryover or a grace period, but not both.[18] For more information, see the "Grace periods" section later in this chapter.

FSAs must adhere to the uniform coverage rule,[19] which requires that "the maximum amount of reimbursement from a Health FSA must be available at all times during the period of coverage (properly reduced as of any particular time for prior reimbursements for the same coverage period)."[20] In certain limited situations, the Health FSA may be a better option if you have extremely high healthcare expenses in the first part of the plan year. Several versions of FSAs exist; check with your employer to find out which option(s) they offer.

---

17   When we say FSA, we mean health FSA, not dependent care FSA.
18   https://www.irs.gov/pub/irs-drop/n-13-71.pdf
19   Proposed Regulation §1.125-5(d)
20   Prop. Treas. Reg. §1.125-5(d)(1) and IRS Chief Counsel Advice 201107026 (Jan. 6, 2010).

Let's look at a couple of examples.

Examples: HSAs with and without matching funds

Essie and her husband both have access to a Health FSA. Essie had a heart transplant a number of years ago and meets her HSA-qualified HDHP's out-of-pocket maximum of $5,500 every year in February. She and her husband can both contribute $2,750 to their Health FSAs, for a total of $5,500 for the year. Essie's employer does not make HSA contributions. Because Essie and her husband are struggling financially right now, they decide that having each of them contribute the maximum to the Health FSA will be better for them financially. Essie can be reimbursed for their total out-of-pocket expenses as she submits claims for them, even though she and her husband have not yet contributed the full amount.

The next year, Essie's employer puts in a match of $2 for every dollar contributed to an HSA and adds a feature that allows Essie to advance her employer contributions should she need them before they are deposited. Essie and her husband decide to open an HSA and contribute the family maximum of $7,200. In 2021 Essie will contribute $2,400 and her employer will match it with an additional $4,800 for a total of $7,200. This allows Essie and her husband to meet their out-of-pocket maximum of $5,500 but still have a balance of $1,700 in their HSA for future out-of-pocket qualified medical expenses.

HRAs

Some businesses prefer to offer an HRA, which allows them to reimburse employees for eligible medical expenses (which may include copayments, deductibles, vision and dental expenses, prescriptions, and personal insurance policy premiums). Reimbursements are tax-free for the employee and tax-deductible for the employer.

Several varieties of HRAs exist to meet different needs:

- Group Coverage HRA (provides financial assistance to employees towards eligible out-of-pocket expenses)

- Dental/Vision HRA, Limited Purpose HRA, or Post-deductible HRA

- Qualified Small Employer HRA (QSEHRA)

- Individual Coverage HRA (ICHRA)

- Excepted Benefit HRA (EBHRA)

- Retiree HRA

All HRAs follow a similar process:

1. Employer designs plan, defines which employees are eligible, and sets reimbursement limits.

2. Employee incurs healthcare bills.

3. Employee submits claims for reimbursement.

4. Employer reviews claim and reimburses employee, up to the set limit.

HRAs can either stand alone or exist alongside other health benefits, depending on the type of HRA they are. Employers have complete flexibility to customize their HRA plan design. Unused funds may roll over to a subsequent HRA plan year, depending on the plan design. In addition, unused funds may be able to be used post-termination or in retirement, depending on plan design.

Self-employed persons may not participate in an HRA because, unlike HSAs, HRAs cannot be funded by employees.

Specialized accounts

Having a general FSA or HRA can make you ineligible to contribute to an HSA. However, in order to provide FSA or HRA benefits that can be used by employees also covered by an HSA-qualified HDHP, employers can make HSA-qualified versions of these plans available.[21]

To compare various types of HRAs, refer to the following chart. For more details, see the descriptions that follow.

21   Rev. Rul. 2004-45

	HRA	HSA-Qualified HRA	QSEHRA
	HRA	Post-Deductible or Limited Purpose HRA	Qualified Small Employer HRA
General purpose	An HRA to help with out-of-pocket costs	An HRA for HSA owners	HRAs for small businesses
Eligible expenses	Out-of-pocket medical expenses	Either pays dental or vision expenses only or includes out-of-pocket medical expenses once the deductible is met	Out-of-pocket medical expenses
Pays coverage premiums	No	No	Individual and group (group premiums reimbursed after tax)
Compatible with FSA	Yes	Yes	No
Compatible with HSA	No	Yes	Sometimes
Premium Tax Credit (PTC)	Affordable MV coverage disqualifies	No impact	Affordable MV coverage disqualifies
HSA eligibility	Other group health plan coverage required	No impact	QSEHRA not available

	ICHRA	EBHRA	Retiree HRA
	Individual Coverage HRA	Excepted Benefit HRA	Retiree-Only HRA
General purpose	Like QSEHRA, with higher limits		Only for use after retirement
Eligible expenses	Out-of-pocket medical expenses, some premiums	Based on design, but potentially all eligible out-of-pocket medical expenses	Based on design, but potentially all eligible medical expenses
Pays coverage premiums	Individual only	COBRA EBHRA[22] STLDI	No
Compatible with FSA	Yes	Yes	Yes
Compatible with HSA	Sometimes	Sometimes	Sometimes
Premium Tax Credit (PTC)	Affordable MV coverage disqualifies	No impact	Affordable MV coverage disqualifies
HSA eligibility	ICHRA unavailable unless with a restricted FSA	Non-excepted, group health plan required	No impact

HSA-qualified FSA/HRA

An HSA-qualified FSA or HRA can either provide narrower coverage (for example, limited to dental and vision expenses) or can pay for those expenses until the HDHP minimum deductible is met for the year and then pay for all eligible §213(d) expenses.

Limited purpose HRA/FSA

FSAs and HRAs that limit expenses to dental and vision are typically referred to as limited purpose FSAs (LPFSAs) or limited purpose HRAs (LPHRAs) and work in parallel with HSAs insofar as you can draw money from both at the same time to pay for separate expenses. LPFSAs provide the advantage of making all of the money in the account available to you at the start of the plan year, even if you have not made all of your contributions to the account.

In summary, LPFSA features include the following:

- Covers vision and dental expenses before you reach your deductible (and sometimes after you reach it)

- Does not affect HSA eligibility (unlike a health FSA)

- Is funded with pre-tax dollars

It makes sense to contribute to an LPFSA if you choose to contribute the entire allowable yearly maximum to your HSA. The main disadvantage is that you must forfeit all unspent FSA funds at the end of the year, unless your employer provides a grace period or allows you to roll over a portion of the FSA.

Example: Maximizing tax-advantages through an LPFSA

Spencer has an HSA with an LPFSA that covers vision and dental expenses only.

When his wife, Rachel, takes their young son to the dentist, the dentist says they will need a dental appliance to correct a jaw problem. Rachel asks the dentist for a cost estimate for the appliance, as well as for other dental work Spencer will need during the coming year.

Rachel also wants to replace her prescription sunglasses. She contacts several optical shops to compare costs and gets estimates for exams, frames, and lenses.

In 2021, Spencer and Rachel want to maximize their HSA so they can start investing it. Spencer sets up his payroll deductions to contribute the full maximum for a family—$7,200. Then he elects to contribute $2,300 to his FSA (based on the estimates for dental work and glasses).

This equals $9,500 in income Spencer and Rachel are able to protect from taxes.

With the FSA to pay the dental and vision expenses, Spencer and Rachel can invest more of their entire HSA contribution for the year in a mutual fund.

Post-deductible FSA/HRA[23]

Alternatively, an HSA-qualified Health FSA or an HRA can be set up to provide benefits only after the minimum annual deductible specified in the HDHP has been satisfied (these are often referred to as a post-deductible FSA or HRA).

In this case, the FSA or HRA works in cooperation with the HSA. These arrangements cannot pay or reimburse any medical expenses incurred before you meet the minimum HSA-qualified HDHP deductible of $1,400 for single coverage or $2,800 for family coverage in 2021. After that, you can use the account to cover copayments or coinsurance. These accounts, however, can typically be used to cover dental and vision expenses before you meet the deductible. Some post-deductible FSAs or HRAs may be designed to require you to meet your specific HSA-qualified HDHP's deductible rather than the minimums stated above. Be sure to check with your employer so you understand the specific rules of your plan.

If your employer provides an HSA-qualified HDHP with a post-deductible FSA or HRA, you can submit your receipts for reimbursement only after you meet your IRS minimum deductible.

---

23   Rev. Rul. 2004-45

Example: Gap between deductible and out-of-pocket maximum

Toshiko's employer offers an HDHP with a $3,000 deductible and a $4,000 out-of-pocket maximum.

To help close the gap between the plan's deductible and the out-of-pocket maximum, her employer also offers a $500 post-deductible HRA.

Toshiko has a lot of medical expenses during the year and she spends her entire HSA contribution of $3,550. After meeting her deductible and paying her coinsurance, she submits a reimbursement request to her employer and receives $500 from the HRA.

Qualified small employer HRA

Developed in 2017, a QSEHRA (pronounced q-sarah) allows small employers (with fewer than 50 employees) to reimburse employees tax-free for individual health insurance premiums as well as medical expenses (rather than simply provide group insurance[24].) Each employee may choose their own individual health plan. Employees who already have coverage, perhaps through their spouse, can use the allowance to pay for other medical expenses.

Individual coverage HRA

Developed in 2020, an ICHRA (pronounced ick-rah) expands on the QSEHRA by providing higher limits and greater design flexibility. Like a QSEHRA, it allows employers to reimburse employees tax-free for individual health insurance.

ICHRAs provide a couple of advantages over traditional group plans:

- The reimbursement model (sometimes called a "defined contribution") gives employers more control over costs and gives employees more options to choose from. The current model of group insurance, sometimes called a "defined benefit," requires that employers choose a one-size-fits-all plan for the group and limits employees to the option(s) sponsored by the employer.

---

24   IRS Notice 2015-17

- ICHRAs move the responsibility of managing a health plan from the employer to the employee. Instead of getting involved in choices about which doctor networks employees want, employers merely decide which employees qualify and then set monthly allowances and allow the employees to choose their own insurance.

Excepted benefit HRA (EBHRA)

Since 2019, employers can use an EBHRA (pronounced ebb-rah) to provide funds to help cover the cost of vision, dental, or short-term limited-duration insurance premiums. General health insurance premiums are not eligible for reimbursement under an EBHRA. These accounts are limited to $1,800 for 2021.

You do not need to opt in to your employer's group health insurance coverage to be eligible for an EBHRA.

Retiree HRA

A retiree HRA pays or reimburses only those medical expenses incurred after retirement (and no expenses incurred before retirement). In this case, the individual may contribute to the HSA before retirement, but not after the HRA begins to pay or reimburse qualified medical expenses during retirement. Therefore, after retirement, the individual can no longer contribute to the HSA.

Suspended HRA

In order to contribute to your HSA, you can elect to suspend an HRA before the beginning of an HRA coverage period. The HRA does not pay or reimburse the medical expenses incurred during the suspension period, except for preventive care and items listed under other health coverage. When the suspension period ends, you are no longer eligible to make contributions to an HSA.

Other benefits

An Employee Assistance Program (EAP) is an employee benefit that covers all or part of the cost for employees to receive counseling, referrals, and advice in dealing with stressful issues in their lives.[25]

---

25 IRS Notice 2004-50 Q&A 10

An employee covered by an EAP, wellness program, or a disease management plan can still contribute to an HSA—as long as these plans do not provide substantial medical benefits.

Grace period, run-out period, carryover

General-purpose FSA grace period

Some general-purpose health FSAs have a grace period of up to two and a half months after the plan year ends to use balances accumulated in your account during the plan year (a total of 14½ months). Most grace periods let you continue to incur expenses and get reimbursed, while a run-out period only allows reimbursement for expenses incurred during the plan year. Your plan may or may not provide this benefit[26].

You may make HSA contributions during an FSA grace period that spills into the next plan year if you have no money in the general-purpose Health FSA at the end of the prior plan year.[27]

If you still have funds in the general-purpose FSA during the grace period, you cannot begin contributing to your HSA for the current plan year until the first day of the month following the end of the grace period.

If you are enrolled in a general health FSA with a grace period and you decide to enroll in an HSA-qualified plan for the following year, you may not contribute to your HSA until your grace period ends and you have no access to funds remaining in your general Health FSA.

Example 1: General-purpose health FSA with a grace period balance

Vernon ends his traditional plan, general health FSA coverage on December 31, 2020, and opens an HSA-qualified HDHP on January 1, 2021.

---

26   Prop. Treas. Reg. §1.125-1(e)(2007), IRS Notices 2005-42, 2007-22, 2005-86, IRC §223(c)(1)(B)(iii)
27   IRC §223(c)(1)(B)(iii)

Because he still has money in the FSA at the beginning of the new plan year, he cannot begin contributing to his new HSA until after the FSA's grace period ends on March 15, 2021. Because HSA eligibility always begins on the first day of the month, he must wait until April 1, 2021, to make his first HSA contribution.

Example 2: General-purpose FSA with a zero balance

Anita had a traditional health plan and a general health FSA in 2020. She starts her HSA-qualified HDHP and HSA on January 1, 2021. She is still technically covered by her FSA during the grace period until March 15, 2021. However, because she spent her FSA down to zero by December 31, 2020, she can begin contributing to her HSA on January 1, 2021.

Post-deductible FSA grace period

You could lose your eligibility to contribute to an HSA if you have funds in a post-deductible FSA during the FSA grace period.

Example 1: post-deductible health FSA with a balance carried into the grace period

Anna ends her traditional plan, post-deductible Health FSA coverage on December 31, 2020, and opens an HSA-qualified HDHP on January 1, 2021.

Because she still has money in the FSA at the beginning of the new plan year, she cannot begin contributing to her new HSA until after the FSA's grace period ends on March 15, 2021. Because HSA eligibility always begins on the first day of the month, she must wait until April 1, 2021, to make her first HSA contribution.

Example 2: post-deductible health FSA with a zero balance

Sam had a traditional health plan and a post-deductible health FSA in 2020. He starts his HSA-qualified HDHP and HSA on January 1, 2021. He is still technically covered by his FSA during the grace period until March 15, 2021. However, because he spent his FSA down to zero by December 31, 2020, he can begin contributing to his HSA on January 1, 2021.

LPFSA grace period

You do not lose your eligibility to contribute to an HSA if you have funds in an LPFSA during the FSA grace period.

Example: LPFSA with a balance carried into the grace period

Lorenzo had an LPFSA that only covered vision and dental during 2020. On January 1, 2021, he begins his new HSA-qualified HDHP coverage.

Although he still has funds in the FSA during the FSA's grace period in the new plan year, he may contribute to his HSA starting on January 1, 2021, because limited purpose FSAs do not affect HSA eligibility.

FSA carryover

The IRS sets the carryover limit for health FSAs to 20% of the annual salary reduction contribution limit. The limit increased to $550 in 2020 (20% of the $2,750 limit on salary reduction contributions) and remains the same in 2021.

If you have a health FSA with a rollover feature, the unused funds in an FSA will roll over to the following plan year even if you do not select the FSA benefit for the following year. If you have any funds in an FSA, you may not contribute to an HSA.

Summary

- Consumer-driven healthcare includes the following categories of accounts: MSA, Archer MSA, FSA, HRA.

- HRAs come in several varieties: GCHRA, LPHRA, QSEHRA, ICHRA, EBHRA, Retiree HRA.

- The main categories of HSA-qualified HDHP policies are self-only coverage, self-plus-one coverage, and family coverage.

- An FSA may provide either a grace period or carryover (but not both). Each of these options might affect your ability to contribute to an HSA.

CHAPTER 5

Opening an HSA

Chapter overview

To open an HSA, you must enroll in an HSA-qualified HDHP by the first day of the month in which you want to open your account. Then, as soon as you or your employer contributes to an HSA, you can begin incurring qualified expenses and spending from the account.

Choosing a custodian

You cannot simply set aside HSA contributions in a shoebox, safe-deposit box, or ordinary bank account—you can only use an account specifically designated as an HSA.

Role of custodian

The HSA trustee or custodian holds your balances, receives and records contributions, and processes distributions. The custodian also prepares the appropriate tax reporting forms for you at the end of the year.

In general, an insurance company or a bank can be an HSA trustee or custodian, as can any entity approved by the IRS as a trustee or custodian for individual retirement accounts (IRAs). Other entities may request approval to be an HSA trustee or custodian under IRS regulations.

Not all companies provide the same level of service or support. Do your homework about the quality of product and service offered before you sign up with an HSA custodian.

Questions to ask

You may set up an HSA on your own, or your employer may make arrangements for you to establish an HSA with a particular HSA custodian.

Your HDHP and HSA do not have to be managed by the same company; you may prefer the service, terms, and investment opportunities of an HSA custodian independent from your insurance company.

It is important that your expectations for the basic administration of your HSA are clear. Some of the issues you should review include fees, investment earnings, and how your account will be managed. Consider finding the answers to the following questions before selecting a custodian.

Account contributions and management

- How much should I contribute and how often?

- Can I make a contribution monthly, quarterly, or with any payroll?

- What methods can I use to make contributions?

- How often will I receive a statement?

- When and how often can I increase or decrease my contributions?

- When will I receive my debit card and other welcome materials?

- What should I do if I need to use the account before I receive my debit card?

- How should I save and organize my receipts for tax filing and potential disputes?

Fees

The Department of Labor (DOL) requires that custodians provide timely and comprehensive information about any applicable investment fees, in the form of a 404(a)(5) participant fee disclosure. Before selecting a custodian, ask the following questions about fees:

- How are fees set?

- What does the trustee or custodian charge to manage accounts, keep records, and send forms and statements?

- What are fees based on?
  Does the trustee or custodian base fees on the amount in my account or on how much I contribute monthly? Or do I pay a fixed fee, independent of my HSA balance? Does the custodian waive fees if my balance reaches a certain level?

- Which fees are assessed?
  Some possible fees include those for account maintenance, replacement of lost or stolen checks, stop-payment (in the event of a dispute with a healthcare provider or an erroneous charge), rollover, and account closure.

- Who pays the fees?

- If I open an account through my employer, does my employer pay the fees, or do I?

- Can I pay fees directly or do they have to be paid from my account?

- Do fees count against the amount I can spend?

Account earnings

HSA custodians can offer federally insured accounts (Federal Deposit Insurance Corporation, or FDIC or National Credit Union Administration, or NCUA) which earn a modest interest rate while guaranteeing the principal up to the balance limit. Most HSA custodians also offer a platform of self-directed mutual funds—usually publicly traded stocks and bonds, subject to market risk and fluctuation in value over time. The principal balance in mutual funds is not guaranteed and is not FDIC or NCUA insured. Investors should carefully consider information contained in the fund prospectus, including investment objectives, risks, charges, and expenses.

- What is the rate of return on my account?
  For instance, what is the interest rate and how is interest compounded?

- Is it federally insured

- What about making investments?

- Is there a minimum balance threshold in order to make investments?

- Is there a charge to make investments?

- Is there a minimum amount of money that must be invested?

- Does the account carry investment risk?

Account management by trustee or custodian

- Does the trustee or custodian impose limits on the size or number of distributions that I can take during a given period?

- Does the trustee or custodian accept rollovers or trustee-to-trustee transfers from other eligible accounts?
  The law allows trustees and custodians to accept rollovers and transfers but does not require them to.

- How easily can I move money from an investment account back to the HSA if needed for a large medical expense?

- Is there a waiting period?

- Are there extra fees?

- Does the trustee or custodian provide a broad range of investments and investment choices that suit my needs?

Additional services

Sometimes healthcare costs seem confusing or opaque. As an HSA owner, learn how to determine true costs so you can spend your money wisely and maximize your investment.

Some HSA providers offer services to assist you in making wise decisions. Choose an HSA provider that adds value by helping you research healthcare costs so you can save money and spend your healthcare dollars wisely. Consider the following:

- Will I have access to quality cost comparison tools from my employer, health plan, or HSA custodian?

- Does the trustee or custodian provide phone and/or online help to assist me in reviewing and minimizing my healthcare spending?

- When is phone support available? What if I have an emergency in the middle of the night?

- What types of services are provided with a mobile application for my smart phone or tablet?

- Does my custodian provide simple-to-use investment options and advice to help me grow my HSA balance?

- Does my custodian charge me to invest my HSA dollars?

Other considerations

Various HSA custodians offer different investment options and benefits and charge different fees. When selecting an HSA custodian, consider the following:

Investment advice

Automated advice (sometimes called 'robo-advice') is a way to manage investments using computer algorithms or other formulas. The algorithms, controlled by software, do not require a human financial adviser to manage the client's account. If your HSA custodian does provide automated advice, ask how much this service costs and how successful the technology has been with returns on investments.

- Does the HSA provider offer advice on your investments, including automated advice?

Fees

Different providers charge different fee amounts, so clarify their fee structure before choosing an HSA custodian. Lower fees mean you will keep more of your investment earnings while higher fees could dramatically reduce your earnings over time. Consider that funds typically carry underlying fees, which should be considered in your evaluation of the overall cost of investing with a given provider.

- How much does the HSA custodian charge in investment-related fees?

Example: Save vs. invest

Raphael has an HSA-qualified high-deductible family health plan and, after medical expenses, makes a net contribution of $3,000 each year to his HSA. If Raphael saves the same amount every year for 30 years but doesn't invest those dollars, he will accumulate $90,000 over a 30-year period, assuming he is not receiving significant interest on his cash balance. However, if Raphael invests the net contribution of $3,000 each year (after meeting the minimum investment threshold) in a diversified investment portfolio, continually invests the balance and is able to achieve a 7% annualized rate of return, his savings could grow to as much as $306,000—this is, $216,000 more than the actual amount he invested. (Individual results may vary.)

Opening an HSA

You can open your HSA at any time throughout the year if you are already enrolled in an HSA-qualified HDHP, but most people enroll in their HSA during their employer's open enrollment period. Once you qualify to open an HSA, you can keep it, with only continued enrollment in an HSA-qualified health plan (and no other disqualifying coverage) required to continue making contributions to your HSA.

Enrollment

In most cases, you will enroll through your employee benefits or HR website.

If you open an HSA independent of your employer, then the HSA provider you select may have an online enrollment process. If you open an HSA at a bank, you can enroll in person or on the bank's website. If you use an insurance broker, they will have forms or websites to help you enroll in an HSA.

Custodial agreements

Your HSA custodian will require that you sign a custodial agreement or a trust agreement, or otherwise enroll as part of your employer-based health insurance program. If you enroll in an HSA as part of an online HDHP enrollment process, you may not need to sign a physical form.

IRS Form 5305-B and 5305-C shows what a trust or custodial agreement looks like.

Customer Identification Program (CIP)

As part of the USA Patriot Act, an individual opening any sort of financial account (in this instance, an HSA) undergoes a verification process, which includes name, date of birth, Social Security Number (SSN), and address.[1]

Beneficiaries

When you open an HSA, designate a beneficiary. If you designate your spouse, ownership of the HSA will transfer to him or her upon your death as a tax-advantaged HSA. For other named beneficiaries, the fair market value of the HSA becomes part of your estate and becomes taxable income for the beneficiary when distributed.

Payment methods

Many HSA administrators provide a debit card or checkbook with which to pay qualified medical expenses from your HSA.

Doctors and other healthcare providers may ask you to pay at the time of your visit or, if you use a network provider, they may send the bill to your insurance company for repricing and then send you the adjusted bill.

Ask your healthcare provider to contact your health plan for claim submission information to have your health plan pay any qualified medical expenses and then decide whether to use your HSA for the portion that is your responsibility. Your HSA custodian and your health plan can assist you if you have questions.

---

1   HR 3162, Public Law 107-56

Who can establish and contribute to an HSA?

The IRS has specific guidelines to determine who is eligible to open and contribute to an HSA. Once you are eligible to open an HSA, it remains yours, even if you no longer have an HDHP. Eligibility is only required to make contributions to the account.

Definition of an eligible individual

Under the law, an eligible individual:

- Must be covered under a qualified HDHP on the first day of any month for which eligibility is claimed.[2]

- May not be covered under any health plan that would disqualify you from having an HSA, with the exception of certain permitted coverage and certain health-related payment plans discussed in Chapter 2.

- Must not be enrolled in Medicare (the healthcare component of the Social Security program).[3]

- May not be claimed as a dependent on another individual's tax return.[4]

Healthcare reform and adult children

Under the Patient Protection and Affordable Care Act (PPACA), adult children up to the age of 26 can be covered by their parents' HSA-qualified HDHP, but their medical expenses may not be able to be paid from their parents' HSA (see the "Who does your HSA cover" section later in this chapter).

You may choose to cover your adult child until they turn 26, even if he or she:

- Gets married

- Has a baby or adopts a child

- Attends school (or not)

---

2   IRC §223(a), IRS Notice 2004-2 Q&A 2 through Q&A 7
3   IRC §223(b)(7), IRS Notice 2004-50 Q&A 2 through Q&A 4
4   IRC §223(b)(6)

- Does not live with you

- Qualifies for health coverage through their job

If your adult child is self-supporting or does not qualify as a tax deduction, that child's healthcare expenses cannot be reimbursed from the parent's HSA.[5] However, single adult children who are not tax dependents and who have coverage under a parent's family HSA-qualified HDHP can open their own HSAs and contribute up to the annual family maximum: $7,200 for 2021 or $7,300 for 2022.[6]

Anyone can contribute to the adult child's HSA, even their parents, provided the balance does not exceed the legal annual contribution limit. Your adult child can use his or her own HSA to pay for qualified medical expenses incurred by their spouse and tax dependents.

In other words, parents of adult children may contribute the family maximum to their own HSA. Also they (or their children) can contribute the family maximum to their adult children's HSAs as well. You do not have to split the maximum family contribution limit with the children, as you would with a spouse.

If you give your adult child an HSA, you do not get to deduct the contribution, but your child receives the contribution tax-free.[7]

Employed individuals

Employers typically pay a portion of the premiums for employee health plan options and an employer who offers an HSA-qualified HDHP may pay for some or all of the premiums and may also contribute toward an HSA because their costs for premiums are typically lower than those of other health plans. Even if the employer contributes, the participant owns the HSA funds.

Employers may have additional requirements for employees who want to participate in any offered health plan, including a certain length of employment or a minimum number of hours, so be sure you understand your employer's eligibility requirements to reduce misunderstandings and confusion.

5   IRC §223(d)(2), IRC §152, PHS §2714, which adds the age 26 rule for medical insurance
6   IRC §223(b)(6), IRS Notice 2004-2 Q&A 18
7   IRS Notice 2004-2 Q&A 18

Self-employed individuals

Even subchapter S owners or self-employed individuals can open an HSA and make contributions as long as all IRS eligibility requirements are met.

As a 2-percent shareholder-employee in an S corporation, you are not considered an employee and cannot contribute to an HSA through the cafeteria plan under IRC §125. But, you can make HSA contributions and deduct them on your taxes.[8]

Retired and disabled individuals

If an otherwise eligible person is not enrolled in Medicare even though that individual has reached age 65, he or she can contribute to an HSA until the month they are enrolled in Medicare.[9] The individual may also make catch-up contributions prior to their enrollment in Medicare.[10]

Regardless of your age, you may still set up and contribute to an HSA as long as you have an HSA-qualified HDHP and are not enrolled in Medicare.

If you have an HSA-qualified HDHP as well as access to a retiree HRA that provides reimbursement only after you retire, you may still set up an HSA as long as you are not enrolled in Medicare.[11]

If you are covered by an HSA-qualified HDHP/HSA combination and qualify for short-term or long-term disability benefits under an employer-sponsored plan, nothing should change if the basic healthcare coverage arrangement remains intact during the disability period.

If you are receiving Social Security disability benefits, you may lose eligibility to contribute to your HSA when your Medicare coverage begins.

Who does your HSA cover?

Under the law, you can use HSA funds to pay qualified medical expenses for yourself, your spouse, and any dependents claimed on your taxes, and a few other individuals, described below.

---

8   IRC §125(d)(1)(A), IRC §1372, IRC §318
9   IRC §223(b)(7), IRS Notice 2004-50 Q&A 2
10   IRS Notice 2004-50 Q&A 3
11   Rev. Rul. 2004-45 Situation 5

You and your spouse

You can pay your spouse's qualified medical expenses from your HSA whether or not your spouse is covered by an HSA-qualified HDHP.

Even if both spouses have an HSA, one spouse can pay for qualified medical expenses for the other.

You can also use HSA funds to pay the qualified medical expenses of same-sex spouses, but not domestic partners unless they qualify as dependents for tax purposes.[12]

Example: Paying expenses for spouse not covered by an HDHP

Paul has a traditional plan that does not meet the criteria for an HSA-qualified HDHP (because his plan has first-dollar coverage that requires copayment) and does not cover Sean, his husband.

Sean elects an HSA-qualified HDHP and HSA for himself.

Even though Paul is not covered by Sean's HSA-qualified HDHP, Sean can use his HSA to pay Paul's copayments.[13]

Your dependents

Who counts as a dependent for family coverage? According to the PPACA, any dependent you include on your tax return counts as a dependent for health plan purposes. In fact, you must make certain that everyone included on your tax return has coverage—even if you do not pay for it yourself.

Whose medical expenses can you pay from your HSA? According to IRS Publication 969,[14] you can pay the qualified medical expenses of anyone you claim as a dependent on your tax return, as well as the expenses of some other people who don't quite qualify as your tax dependents.

---

12   IRS Notice 2014-1
13   IRS Notice 2004-50 Q&A 36
14   https://www.irs.gov/pub/irs-pdf/p969.pdf

Dependents claimed on tax return

A person claimed as a dependent for both income tax and health plan purposes must bear a relationship to the taxpayer or policy holder in one of the following ways:[15]

- Child (including a legally adopted or foster child), grandchild, or great-grandchild

- Stepchild or your stepchild's descendant

- Sibling, half-sibling, step-sibling, or a descendant of these

- Parent, grandparent, or other direct blood ancestor

- Stepfather or stepmother

- Brother or sister of your father or mother

- Descendant of your brother or sister

- Father-in-law, mother-in-law, son-in-law, daughter-in-law, brother-in-law, or sister-in-law

Tax dependents must also meet other stipulations, not included here, that do not apply to those considered dependents for health plan purposes.

Other dependents

In addition to your spouse and tax dependents, you may cover the qualified medical expenses of a few other people (adult children or other relatives) who come close to the definition of a tax dependent, but fall short for one of two reasons:[16]

- A relative who has a gross income higher than the IRS-determined limit ($4,300 in 2021).

- A child or relative who files a joint return.

In addition, your dependents can pay for their dependents' qualified medical expenses, even though you claim them as a dependent on your tax return.

---

15   IRC §152, IRS Notice 2008-5
16   IRC §223(d)(2)(A); IRC §223(d)(2); IRS Notice 2008-59 Q&A 33, IRS Pub 969; IRC §152, PHS §2714

Example 1: Married child covered by parents' HSA

Your 19-year-old daughter, Sarah, and her husband, Richard, live with you. You provide more than half of her support. Even though they file jointly and earn more than $4,300, you can pay her qualified medical expenses out of your HSA.

Example 2: HSA owner claimed as a tax dependent

Your 20-year-old daughter, Mary Alice (a full-time student), her husband, Robert, and their baby, Dory, live with you. Even though you claim Mary Alice as a tax dependent, Robert can pay Mary Alice's qualified medical expenses from his own HSA.

In general, you can cover more people with your health plan than you can cover with your HSA. For example, you can include your adult children in your family coverage until they're 26, but can only pay their expenses from your HSA if they qualify as a dependent for tax purposes (under 19, or under 24 if in school full time).

Likewise, your HSA can pay the qualified medical expenses of a broader variety of people than you can claim as tax dependents. For example, you can pay the expenses of a married adult child who files a joint return if they are younger than 19 (or a full-time student younger than 24).

In a nutshell, your HSA funds generally cover the expenses incurred by your spouse and tax dependents, with a couple of possible additions.

Summary

- You need to enroll in an HSA-qualified HDHP in order to open an HSA. In order to qualify, the plan must adhere to government-mandated minimum annual deductibles and out-of-pocket maximums. These two limits change from time to time.

- You can choose one of several types of custodians for your HSA—usually an insurance company or bank. The custodian will oversee contributions and distributions and provide statements and tax paperwork.

- To open an HSA, you must enroll in an HSA-qualified HDHP by the first day of the month in which you want to open your account. In other words, if you are covered by your HSA-qualified HDHP on August 1, you can also open the HSA in August. If you are covered by your HSA-qualified HDHP beginning on August 2, you need to wait until September 1 to open your HSA.

- Your HSA can be used to pay qualified medical expenses for any dependents you claim on your taxes, even though your health coverage (HSA-qualified HDHP) may cover dependents who you cannot claim for tax purposes, including children between the ages of 19 and 26 as well as dependents whom you do not financially support.

- Even though you cannot use your HSA to pay the expenses of adult children who are not your tax dependents, they may open an HSA for themselves if they are covered by an HSA-qualified HDHP (their own or their parents').

- Update your HSA beneficiary to avoid confusion and unnecessary taxes for your heirs when you die.

CHAPTER 6

Contributing to an HSA

Chapter overview

Your contributions are protected from state (in most states) and federal income tax. In addition, the government provides generous contribution rules for HSAs.

- Anyone (employer, family member, or any other person) may contribute to an HSA on behalf of an eligible HSA holder.

- Each year, the maximum allowable contribution increases slightly, indexed to inflation.

- Even if you open an HSA mid-year, you can still contribute the entire annual maximum amount, provided you remain eligible for the next year.

- Rollovers and transfers do not contribute to your annual contribution limit, with some restrictions.

Tax breaks and ownership

You never pay federal income tax on the money in your HSA—not when you contribute, realize growth, or even spend the money, provided you use the account only for qualified medical expenses. Even if you contribute using taxable income (for example, if you have an HSA not associated with your employer's health plan), your contributions are included as an above-the-line deduction when you file your federal income tax return, reducing your taxable income whether or not you itemize deductions.[1]

Although nearly anyone can contribute to your HSA, only you (and your employer) can claim a tax deduction on contributions. Others who contribute to your account may not take a tax deduction, but their contributions to your HSA do not add to your gross income.[2]

Employer contributions also do not affect your potential eligibility for the earned income credit (EIC).[3]

Because self-employed individuals and 2% owners of S corporations are not considered employees, they cannot receive "employer" contributions to their HSA from their business. However, they can make personal contributions and claim the above-the-line deduction on their income taxes.

HSA ownership

Because you own all of the funds in your HSA, if your company is sued or files for bankruptcy your employer's creditors cannot touch these funds. (Though in the event of personal bankruptcy or divorce, creditors can likely access the funds in your HSA.) In addition, the law protects your account's beneficiaries.

Unused money in your HSA rolls over year-to-year and is fully portable, which means you can take the account with you if you leave your employer, if your employer changes health plans, or if you change health plans.

---

1   IRS Notice 2004-2 Q&A 17
2   IRS Notice 2004-2 Q&A 18 and 19
3   IRS Notice 2004-50 Q&A 85

Finally, an employer cannot recoup any money they previously contributed to your HSA and then only under certain circumstances and rules.[4,5]

Example: Employee quits before end of the first year

Reuben's employer contributed $2,000 to his HSA on January 1 expecting that he would work through December 31. Reuben terminated his employment on May 3, but his employer may not recoup any portion of its contribution to Reuben's HSA.

Example: Contribution is made to the incorrect employee

John Smith's employer contributed $2,000 to his HSA on January 1. However, the contribution was intended for John Smyth. John's employer may fix the mistaken contribution, recouping it from Smith's account and making the contribution to Smyth's HSA instead.

Contribution limits

The IRS determines the maximum amount you can contribute to your HSA every year. These limits apply to the total amount added to the HSA during the year, from all sources.

HSA holders and employers can contribute less, if desired.

HSA contribution limit	2021	2022
Individual	$3,600	$3,650
Family	$7,200	$7,300
Additional catch-up contribution for those 55 and older	$1,000	$1,000

---

4   IRC §223(d)(1)(E), IRS Notice 2004-50 Q&A 81
5   IRS Notice 2008-59 and IRS Informational Letter 2018-0033 (September 9, 2015)

Example: Employer contributes to employee's HSA

Jerome and Taneesha are married and have a qualified HDHP with a family deductible of $3,500 effective January 1, 2021.

Jerome's employer contributes $85 per month to his HSA, for a total of $1,020 per year.

Because Jerome's 2021 HSA contribution limit is $7,200, he can contribute (or receive contributions from others) up to $6,180—though he can choose to contribute less than that, or even nothing at all.

Age-related considerations

55 and older[6]

Individuals 55 and older can make catch-up contributions to their HSAs.

HSA owners age 55 and older can make an additional $1,000 contribution to increase their account balance before retirement.

If each spouse is 55 or older, then both spouses must have their own HSA to make catch-up contributions on behalf of both people. A married couple with two HSAs may make catch-up contributions totaling $2,000 in 2021 and 2022.[7]

Example: Married couple makes catch-up contributions

If Roger and Noelle are both older than 55, are eligible for HSAs, and neither is covered by Medicare, then they can contribute an additional $2,000 ($1,000 each) to their individual HSAs for 2021 and 2022. If only Roger has an HSA, he can contribute an extra $1,000 as a catch-up contribution. Noelle could also establish her own HSA and make her catch-up contribution to her account.

---

6   RC §223(b)(3)
7   IRS Notice 2004-2 Q&A 14

Medicare enrollment

All contributions must cease once you enroll in Medicare. Though you can't contribute to the HSA, you can continue to invest the money in your account and take distributions for qualified medical expenses.

If you delay your enrollment in Medicare, you can continue to make contributions (including catch-up contributions) past the age of 65, provided you still have an HSA-qualified HDHP and no other disqualifying coverage.[8]

Opening an HSA mid-year

New account holders who enroll in an HSA-qualified HDHP and open an HSA mid-year may either contribute a prorated amount (for the actual number of months they are eligible) or take advantage of the IRS full-contribution rule and contribute the entire yearly maximum for their age and level of coverage.

Some life changes, described in the "Family changes" section later in the chapter, also affect contribution decisions.

Prorating the contribution

If you are not certain that you will still be enrolled in your HDHP during the entire next tax year, then you can contribute a prorated amount for the months you are actually eligible in the current tax year.

To do this, divide the yearly allowable maximum contribution by 12, then multiply the result by the number of months you are eligible during this tax year.

Example: Contributing a prorated amount

Carlos starts a new job in September and enrolls as an individual in his company's qualified HDHP on October 1, 2021, but his assignment will not be considered permanent until the end of his company's standard six-month probationary period.

Carlos wants to contribute as much as possible to his HSA, but there are only three months left in the year and he has no guarantee that he will be employed and covered by his HDHP the entire following year.

8   IRS Notice 2004-50 Q&A 2

Carlos decides to prorate his contribution for the months he is actually enrolled in the HDHP in the current year.

He divides his yearly maximum contribution by 12.

$$\$3,600 \div 12 \text{ months} = \$300/\text{month}$$

He multiplies the prorated amount by the number of months he will be eligible to determine the amount he can safely contribute without penalty in the event he does not have the opportunity to enroll in an HSA-qualified HDHP next year.

$$\$300 \times 3 \text{ months} = \$900$$

Applying the full contribution rule

The full-contribution rule (or last-month rule) allows individuals who are eligible to contribute to an HSA on the first day of the last month of their tax year (December 1 for most taxpayers) to be considered eligible for the entire year, allowing them to contribute up to their full yearly maximum.

For example, if an individual first becomes eligible for an HSA on December 1, 2021, and has family HSA-qualified HDHP coverage, for purposes of HSA contribution limits, he or she is considered to have had family HDHP coverage for all 12 months of 2021.

The full contribution rule also applies to catch-up contributions for individuals age 55 and older.

The full-contribution rule applies regardless of whether the individual was eligible for the entire year, had HSA-qualified HDHP coverage for the entire year, or had disqualifying non-HDHP coverage for part of the year.

However, a testing period applies for purposes of the full-contribution rule. In general, if you fail to maintain an HSA-qualified HDHP during the entire testing period (usually the full next plan year), you will have to pay taxes and penalties for making an excess contribution. For more details, see the next section.

Example: Using the full-contribution rule

Roberto's HSA-qualified HDHP coverage starts on November 10, 2021. Because he has HSA-qualified HDHP coverage by December 1, he can contribute $3,600 to his HSA, as if he had qualifying coverage for the entire year.

Karl is covered by his HSA-qualified HDHP on November 30, 2021 but waits until February 1, 2022, to open his HSA. The IRS allows account holders to make 2021 contributions until April 15, 2022, so Karl makes a lump sum contribution of $3,600 for 2021. He also starts contributing for 2022 by setting up regular payroll deductions.

Nancy joins her HSA-qualified HDHP on December 2, 2021. She cannot make a full-year contribution for 2021, like Roberto and Karl, because she missed the December 1 deadline for being in an HSA-qualified HDHP. In fact, she cannot contribute for the month of December, because she has to be in an HSA-qualified HDHP on the first day of the month in which she makes a contribution to her HSA. She cannot contribute to her HSA until January 1, 2022.

Testing period

Under the full-contribution rule, the testing period begins with the last month of your tax year and ends on the last day of the twelfth month following that month (for example, December 1, 2021, through December 31, 2022.)

If you contributed to your HSA under the full-contribution rule, then you must remain HSA eligible for the entire testing period. If you fail to remain eligible during the entire testing period (except by death or disability), you must pay taxes on the excess contribution, as well as a 10% penalty.

To determine the excess amount, use the following formula:

Determine the per-month prorated amount by dividing the yearly maximum contribution by 12.

Multiply the monthly amount by the number of eligible months in the year the full-contribution rule applied.

Subtract this number from the amount of the contribution made to determine how much the government will reclassify as income.

Example 1: Eligible for only part of the testing period

Chris, age 53, becomes an eligible individual on December 1, 2021. He has family HSA-qualified HDHP coverage. Under the full-contribution rule, he contributes $7,200 to his HSA for 2021.

Chris loses his eligibility in June 2022 when he drops his HSA-qualified HDHP coverage. Because Chris does not remain an eligible individual during the testing period (December 1, 2021, through December 31, 2022), the contributions made in 2021 that would not have been made without the full-contribution rule must be included in his 2022 income, the year he became ineligible (not 2021, the year in which he made the excess contribution).

Chris uses the worksheet for line 3 of IRS Form 8889 instructions to determine this amount.

January	0
February	0
March	0
April	0
May	0
June	0
July	0
August	0
September	0
October	0
November	0
December	$7,200
Total for all months	$7,200
Total for one month	$600

Chris includes $6,600 ($7,200 minus the $600 that was allowed for the one month he was eligible in 2021) in his gross income on his 2022 tax return. Also, an additional 10% tax ($660) applies to the $6,600 he over-contributed in 2021.

Example 2: Eligible for only part of the testing period

Sixty-year-old Lian started a new job and enrolled in her HDHP and HSA on June 1, 2021.

Because she plans to retire in five years, she wants to contribute as much as she can to her retirement accounts. She decides to take advantage of the full-contribution rule and contributes the maximum annual amount in her HSA ($3,600 + catch-up contribution of $1,000 = $4,600). Because her new job begins on June 1, Lian will be in a qualified HDHP for seven months in 2021.

Lian needs to remain in a qualified HDHP until December 31, 2022 to avoid taxes and penalties on the extra amount she contributes in 2021. Unfortunately, Lian's employer lays her off in March 2022.

Because Lian does not stay in her employer's HDHP for the entire testing period (December 1, 2021 through December 31, 2022), she must pay income tax and a 10% excise tax on the amount she over-contributed in 2021. To calculate the amount she has to reclassify as taxable income, she divides the amount she contributed in 2021 by 12 to find the prorated monthly amount.

$$\$4,600/12 = \$383.33$$

Then, she multiplies the monthly prorated amount by five to calculate the amount she overcontributed (for the five months she was not enrolled in an HDHP in 2021):

$$5 \times \$383.33 = \$1,916.67$$

She prepares to add $1,916.67 to her adjusted gross income on her 2022 tax return and pay an additional 10% tax ($191.67) but finds out she doesn't need to. By continuing her HDHP coverage under COBRA until December 31, 2022, she satisfies the testing period. In addition, the law allows Lian to use her HSA funds to pay the COBRA premiums.[9]

---

9   IRC §223(d)(2)(C)(i), IRS Notice 2004-2 Q&A 27

By purchasing COBRA coverage, she not only avoids additional tax and penalty, but she also continues her health insurance coverage throughout the rest of 2022, even though she was still unemployed.

Two factors contributed to making this option more affordable: She maximized her HSA balance and she probably paid lower COBRA premiums, because HDHP premiums are lower than those for traditional low-deductible health plans.

Eligibility and timing of contributions

Eligibility determined monthly

Eligibility to contribute to an HSA is determined on a monthly basis.

- Participants must be enrolled in an HSA-qualified HDHP on the first day of the month in order to make contributions to or receive funds from their HSA during that month.[10]

- Unless contributing under the full-contribution rule (see the previous section), you can only make HSA contributions for the months you are covered by an HSA-qualified HDHP.

Contributions tied to the tax year

You will report HSA contributions on your individual tax return, so contribution limits align with the tax year, not with when coverage begins or when the insurance plan year begins. For example, you cannot make 2022 tax year contributions before the start of that tax year, nor after the legal tax year deadline, without extensions.[11]

Most individuals pay their taxes based on the calendar year; therefore, they can make contributions between January 1 of a given year and April 15 of the following year.

Even though your health coverage plan year may last for only 12 months, the schedule for HSA contributions (and dispersals) aligns with the tax year.

Within each tax year, you have flexibility in deciding when to make contributions. You can spread them throughout the year or make them all at once. Both you and your employer can make contributions of any size at any time during the tax year, so long as the combined contributions do not exceed the legal limit.

10 IRC §223(c)(1)(A)
11 IRS Notice 2004-2 Q&A 21

Example: Front-loading the HSA early in the year

Miles and Donetta's doctor predicts that their first baby will be born early in the year, with a gastrointestinal defect that will require a multi-week stay in the neonatal intensive care unit (NICU).

Their hospital will require that they pay the entire out-of-pocket maximum immediately upon their child's birth. If they do not have enough money in their HSA at that time, they will have to make those payments with post-tax (non-HSA) dollars.

Donetta is able to work until a month before the baby's birth.

She and Miles decided to contribute her entire paycheck to their HSA, up to the 2022 limit of $7,300.

When the baby is born, they pay their deductible and coinsurance from their HSA, until their out-of-pocket maximum is met, at which time their HSA-qualified HDHP pays 100% of their remaining expenses.

Miles compares their expenses with what they would have paid without the HSA. Taking into account premiums, coinsurance, deductibles, tax savings, and the interest they would have paid if they financed their portion of the bill with the hospital, they spent significantly less than they would have under their previous traditional, low-deductible PPO plan.

Multiple HSAs

If you have more than one HSA (for example, if you open a new account with a new employer, rather than rolling over your existing HSA), your total yearly contributions to your HSAs combined cannot be more than the IRS-mandated limits.

Family changes

Adding a spouse or child

If you get married, have a baby, or adopt a child, your healthcare coverage needs may change. Under the Health Insurance Portability and Accountability Act (HIPAA), you have the right to ask your plan to cover new family members without waiting for the plan's open enrollment period. (See Appendix A for more information on HIPAA.)

Enrolling a new spouse or baby in your plan

Enroll new family members in your plan as soon as possible. If you switch from an individual plan to family coverage, your allowable HSA contribution increases on the first day of the first full month after you elect HSA-qualified family coverage. You may either make a prorated increase in your contributions for the year or contribute the family maximum for the year in one lump sum, if you believe you will stay in a family plan through the testing period.

Stepchildren

You can typically cover a stepchild in your employer's plan, even if you have not formally adopted him or her. The child has to live with you in a parent-child relationship, and you must support him or her financially. Some plans require that you or your current spouse claim the child as a dependent for tax purposes in order to enroll the child in your plan.

As with adding a newborn, adding a stepchild to your HSA-qualified plan may allow you to increase your HSA contribution. When determining the best way to cover a stepchild, consider the options under your plan as well as those available to your spouse or partner.

Spouse loses coverage

Having a baby may not be the only reason you may need to change from self-only to family coverage.

If you have self-only coverage and your spouse loses coverage, you can change to HSA-qualified family coverage without waiting for your open enrollment period, if your employer allows. As in the case of a new child, your allowable HSA contribution also changes on the first day of the month during which your spouse becomes covered by your HSA-qualified HDHP.

Example: Spouse's family coverage disqualifies the HSA

Alfonso and Muriel each have self-only coverage through their employers. Alfonso has an HSA-qualified HDHP, while Muriel has a traditional plan with a low deductible that does not qualify as an HDHP.

Muriel acquires custody of her daughter, Felicia, who comes to live with them.

Muriel wants to cover Felicia under her plan. However, her plan only offers self-only and family coverage. If she elects family coverage, Alfonso will no longer be able to contribute to an HSA, since he will be covered under her plan, which is disqualifying coverage for HSA purposes.

If Alfonso's plan offers different options, such as self-plus-child, it may save money for him to cover Felicia under his plan.

Spouse has HDHP and an HSA

If you and your spouse have self-only HSA-qualified HDHPs under separate plans, you can each open an HSA and contribute the yearly maximum for an individual.

If either spouse has HSA-qualified family HDHP coverage and the other spouse does not have disqualifying coverage, you are both treated as having family HDHP coverage for annual contribution purposes.

If each spouse has an HSA and family coverage under separate plans, you and your spouse can split the annual contribution limit for families between you--equally or however you choose, provided your total contributions do not exceed the annual maximum. HSA contribution limits for families are $7,200 in 2021 and $7,300 in 2022.[12]

Each spouse 55 and older (and not enrolled in Medicare) can contribute an additional $1,000 catch-up contribution, whether enrolled in family or individual HSA-qualified HDHPs, provided they each have an HSA. Some HSA custodians will open the additional HSA for no additional cost.

---

12 IRC §223(b)(3)(B)

Adult children

Adult children aging out

Once your child turns 26 and transitions off of your plan to his or her own plan, you and your child can both contribute to your child's HSA if the child retains HSA-qualified HDHP coverage. While they received coverage under their parents' HDHP, they could contribute up to the family maximum; when they receive their own coverage, their contribution limit depends on whether they have self-only or family coverage. (For more information about adult children, see the "Who can establish and contribute to an HSA" section in Chapter 5.)

You make contributions to your children's HSAs with post-tax dollars, but your contributions do not increase your child's taxable income because they can claim the HSA contributions you make as an above-the-line income tax deduction.

Example: Adult child ages off parents' HSA-qualified coverage

Lana has been covered under her parents' HSA-qualified HDHP but is no longer eligible because she has aged out. She has not been their tax dependent for several years, but has had her own HSA to which she and her parents contributed the family limit of $7,200 for 2021. She begins coverage under her own, self-only HSA-qualified HDHP beginning in January of 2022. She (and her parents, if they wish) can contribute toward Lana's HSA, up to the self-only annual limit of $3,650.

Legal separation and divorce

Spouses do not jointly own an HSA; each must qualify to contribute to an HSA. In the event of a divorce or legal separation, the HSA owned by one spouse may be divided or given in part or in full to the other spouse by court judgment.

Changing from family to self-only HSA-qualified HDHP coverage

If you made the maximum family contribution to your HSA and keep your family coverage after divorce or legal separation, you will not risk making excess contributions.

However, if you and your spouse were covered by a family HSA-qualified HDHP and you change to self-only coverage after your divorce, you may have to pay income tax and penalties on your excess contributions. In addition, you may have to adjust your contributions to ensure you do not over-contribute in the future. Talk to your tax preparer about how to deal with additional taxes and penalties related to potential excess contributions.

If you made a maximum yearly contribution for a family under the full-contribution rule, divorced mid-year, and changed your coverage to self-only under your health plan's HSA-qualified HDHP, you will fail the testing period for eligibility under family coverage. Either return the excess contribution before the tax filing deadline or include the amount in your gross income and pay a 10% penalty on the amount.

For more information about the testing period, see the "Testing period" section earlier in this chapter.

Avoiding excise tax

You may withdraw some or all of the excess contributions and not pay the applicable excise tax if you withdraw both the excess contribution and the interest earned before the tax deadline. You must still pay income tax on the excess amount.

Include the excess contributions and interest earned as "other income" on your tax return for the tax year you withdraw the contributions and earnings[13]. Note that states might levy separate excise taxes.

For more information about returning excess contributions, see the "Penalties" section at the end of this chapter.

Example: Changing to single coverage during testing period

Janetta, age 41, enrolls with family coverage in her HSA-qualified HDHP on October 1, 2020. Her husband, Jacob, a freelance cabinet maker, does not have his own insurance, so Janetta puts him on her plan. They have no children.

---

13   IRC §223(f)(3)

Although she enrolls in her HSA-qualified HDHP late in the plan year, she is eligible to contribute on December 1, 2020, and makes the maximum family contribution of $7,100 under the full-contribution rule.

Janetta and Jacob divorce in September 2021. In the divorce settlement, Janetta keeps her HSA and changes her HSA-qualified HDHP to self-only coverage. Although she fulfilled the testing period by remaining in an HSA-qualified HDHP, she does not fulfill the testing period for family coverage.

After the divorce, Janetta is eligible for the maximum contribution for a single person under the full-contribution rule.

To determine her excess contribution for 2020, she subtracts the maximum contribution for single-only coverage ($3,550) from the $7,100 family contribution:

$$\$7,100 - \$3,550 = \$3,550$$

On her 2020 tax return, Janetta adds the excess $3,550 to her adjusted gross income and pays an additional 10% tax on that amount.

In January 2021, Janetta makes a lump sum contribution of $7,200 thinking she will have family coverage all year. Because she is still eligible for family coverage on September 1, 2021, she can make nine months of family contributions.

She divides $7,200 and $3,600 by 12 to get the prorated monthly contribution for family and single-only coverage.

Family prorated monthly contribution: **$7,200/12 = $600**
Single-only prorated monthly contribution: **$3,600/12 = $300**

She multiplies the family monthly contribution by nine to get the amount of family-level contributions she can contribute during 2021. Then she does the same for the single-level contributions for the three months after her divorce.

She adds the two amounts to get her maximum allowable contribution for the 2021:

$$\$600 \times 9 = \$5,400$$
$$\$300 \times 3 = \$900$$
$$\$5,400 + \$900 = \$6,300$$

Then she subtracts the amount from the $7,200 she had contributed to find out her excess contribution for 2021:

$$\$7,200 - \$6,300 = \$900$$

Janetta adds the $900 to her adjusted gross income on her 2021 return and pays the 6% excise tax for the excess contribution (the penalty is 6% instead of 10% because she did not make the overcontribution under the full-contribution rule).

COBRA coverage for the divorced spouse[14]

If you and your spouse are both covered under a family plan through one of your employers and you get divorced, the spouse who is not employed by the plan's sponsor may be entitled to buy COBRA continuation coverage under the plan. For more information about COBRA, see the U.S. Department of Labor site, (www.dol.gov/ebsa/faqs/faq-consumer-cobra.html.)

Divorce is a qualifying COBRA event. Those eligible may be required to pay up to 102% of the employer's cost of coverage for COBRA and are entitled to coverage for a limited period of time (from 18 to 36 months, depending on the qualifying event).

The eligibility period may, in some cases, be extended if another qualifying event occurs during the period of COBRA eligibility.

Transfers between tax-advantaged accounts

Trustee-to-trustee transfers

Trustee-to-trustee transfers are transfers of account balances directly from one trustee or custodian to another.

Transfers from other HSAs or from Archer MSAs into an HSA are permitted, if the same person owns both accounts.[15] You may not transfer money from another individual's HSA—even if belonging to a spouse or other family member.

HSA transfers (which may contain balances accumulated in previous tax years) do not

---

14   26 USC §4980B(f), 26 CFR §54.4980B-1 et seq
15   IRS Notice 2002-4 Q&A 23

affect the current year's contribution limits. This type of transfer has similar rules as moving funds from one IRA to another.

There is no limit to the number of trustee-to-trustee transfers you can make within any 12-month period.

Rollover transfers

Rollovers move funds from one HSA or Archer MSA to another—but the funds are sent to the account holder rather than to the trustee or custodian. The individual has only 60 days to re-deposit the funds into an HSA without incurring taxes or penalties.

Only one rollover can be executed within a 12-month period. Like trustee-to-trustee transfers, the rollover does not apply toward annual contribution limits.[16]

Example: Transferring an HSA to another bank or trustee

Omar has an HSA with $5,000 at Bank A and he wants to transfer the entire balance to an HSA at Bank B.

He can roll over his HSA by withdrawing the balance from Bank A and re-depositing it into Bank B, as long as the two transactions occur within 60 days of each other. He also has the option of requesting a trustee-to-trustee transfer, in which Bank A sends the money directly to Bank B.

Omar may choose either of these options and still make contributions for that tax year, without having to consider the rolled over amount in his yearly limit calculations.

However, if Omar withdraws the money and does not re-deposit it or spend it for qualified healthcare within 60 days, a 20% penalty will apply, and he will have to pay income tax on the amount withdrawn.[17]

---

16   IRC §223(f)(5), IRS Notice 2004-50 Q&A 55
17   IRC §223(f)(4)

IRA transfers[18]

To help fund the HSA, an account holder can make a once-per-lifetime trustee-to-trustee transfer from a traditional or Roth IRA (but not a Simple or SEP IRA) to the HSA. This transfer contributes to the annual contribution limit, and thus is limited to the maximum annual contribution for the year.

The individual must remain an eligible individual for the entire 12-month testing period following the month the transfer occurs. If he or she does not remain eligible, the transferred amount is included as income for tax purposes and incurs an additional 10% penalty.

Contributions by others

Spouses

HSAs occur only as individual accounts—never as joint accounts. Even when a husband and wife both work for the same employer and have the same health coverage, their HSAs and contributions remain completely separate.

The following rules for married people apply only if both spouses are eligible individuals. Contribution limits for spouses depend on the type of coverage each spouse chooses.

- If either spouse has family HDHP coverage (that is, if one spouse covers dependents with their healthcare plan and the other spouse covers only themselves), then both spouses are treated as having HSA-qualified family HDHP coverage.[19]

- If each spouse has family coverage under a separate plan, then the contribution limit for the two of them combined is $7,200 in 2021 ($7,300 in 2022). The contribution limit is split equally between the spouses, unless they agree on a different division.[20]

---

18   IRC §223(b)(4)(C); IRC §408(d)(9); IRS Notice 2008-51
19   IRC §223(b)(5)(A)
20   IRC §223(b)(5)(B)(ii); IRS Notice 2004-50 Q&A 32

- If both spouses are 55 or older, then each spouse may make the $1,000 catch-up contribution. If both spouses meet the age requirement, the total contributions under family coverage cannot be more than $9,200 ($7,200 + $1,000 + $1,000) in 2021 or $9,300 in 2022. Each spouse must make the catch-up contribution to his or her own HSA.

Example: Both spouses have family coverage

Dominick, age 58, and Anika, age 53, are married and each have family coverage under separate HSA-qualified HDHPs.

Because both plans provide family coverage, Dominick and Anika are treated as having coverage under one family plan.

They decide to split the $7,200 maximum family contribution for 2021 equally: Dominick contributes $4,600 to his HSA (half of $7,200, plus a $1,000 catch-up contribution).

Anika can contribute only $3,600 to her HSA (half of the $7,200 annual maximum for a family). Because she is only 53, she cannot make a catch-up contribution.

Dominick and Anika can agree to contribute different amounts, but their total annual 2021 contributions cannot exceed $8,200 ($7,200 + $1,000).

Example: Both spouses have self-only coverage

Bernard, age 35, and Joon, age 33, are married. Each has a self-only HSA-qualified HDHP coverage, and each has an HSA.

Bernard can contribute $3,600 to his HSA in 2021, and Joon can contribute $3,600 to hers.

The same limits apply—whether Bernard and Joon work for different employers, one is self-employed and one is an employee, or both are self-employed.

Example: Only one spouse has qualifying coverage

Darrel and Sabrina are married. Darrel's employer offers an HSA-qualified HDHP. Sabrina's employer offers a traditional PPO plan that does not meet eligibility requirements for an HDHP.

Sabrina elects family coverage, covering Darrel under her non-qualifying plan. Darrel is not eligible to contribute to an HSA because he is covered under Sabrina's traditional plan.

However, if Sabrina elected coverage under her plan solely for herself, or for herself and their children, Darrel could participate in his employer's HSA-qualified HDHP and contribute to his own HSA.

Example: Only one spouse eligible to contribute to HSA

Enrique, age 65, and Felicia, age 56, are married. When Enrique turned 65, he enrolled in Medicare. Enrique and Felicia have separate HSAs, each with self-only coverage.

Enrique can no longer contribute to his HSA, but he can continue to use the funds in either his account or Felicia's to pay qualified medical expenses for either himself or Felicia. He can only use his HSA to pay Medicare premiums[21] (not Felicia's), because she has not yet reached age 65.[22]

Felicia is enrolled in an HSA-qualified HDHP, so she can contribute up to $3,600 to her HSA in 2021 ($3,650 in 2022), plus a catch-up contribution of $1,000 each year, because she is over 55.

Example: Simultaneous family and single coverage

Kirk and Isabel are married. Because he has young children from a previous marriage, Kirk has family coverage under an HSA-qualified HDHP with a $5,000 deductible. Through her employer, Isabel has self-only coverage under an HSA-qualified HDHP with a $2,000 deductible.

Because one spouse has family coverage under an HSA-qualified HDHP that could potentially cover the other spouse, they are seen as having family coverage. Their maximum combined contribution is the IRS statutory amount for family coverage: $7,200 for 2021, to be divided between them as they choose.

They file separate tax returns. Because she has no children of her own to claim as dependents like Kirk does, they determine that they could save the most on taxes if Isabel makes a larger contribution to her HSA. They decide that Isabel will contribute 75% of the yearly maximum ($5,400), and Kirk will contribute 25% ($1,800) to his.

---

21 IRC 223(d)(2)(C)(iv); IRS Notice 2004-2 Q&A 27; IRS Notice 2004-50 Q&A 4, 45; IRS Notice 2008-59 Q&A 29
22 IRS Notice 2008-59 Q&A 30

Business entities

In general, self-employed HSA owners and individuals associated with the entities listed below cannot make pre-tax contributions to their own HSAs, and only sometimes qualify for business tax deductions. The details vary for each entity.

Individuals or sole proprietors

Tax law treats sole proprietors the same as individuals who make their own HSA contributions, in that they can deduct their own HSA contributions and health insurance payments from their personal income tax returns.

They do not, however, receive the business-related tax deduction that employers who contribute to their employees' HSAs usually receive. Therefore, sole proprietors cannot enter contributions to their own HSAs as business expenses on Schedule C, because the contribution does not relate to the self-employed individual's trade or business. In addition, the amount of the contribution does not factor in when determining net earnings from self-employment on Schedule SE.[23]

However, the amounts contributed by the business to its employees do qualify as deductions for Schedule C.

Partnerships and multiple-member LLCs

When a partnership makes a contribution to a partner's HSA in exchange for services rendered, the law considers the contribution "distribution of money to the partner," rather than an employer contribution to an employee's HSA.

As guaranteed payments, they add to the partner's gross income, but may be entered as an above-the-line deduction on the partner's federal income tax return.

The partnership may also deduct these contributions.[24]

S corporations

The IRS treats contributions by an S corporation to the HSA of a 2-percent shareholder-employee in exchange for services rendered as guaranteed payments. Because of this, the S corporation may deduct the contributions but must also include them in the individual's gross income.

---

23   IRS Notice 2004-50 Q&A 84
24   Rev. Rul. 91.26, IRC §§162 and 707

The shareholder-employee may deduct contributions made to their own HSAs on their personal income tax returns.

Because the law treats 2-percent shareholder-employees as self-employed individuals, the rules concerning guaranteed payments for partners apply. (See the previous section.)

Single-member LLCs are treated the same as sole proprietorships.

Penalties

Excess contributions

Excess contributions include any amounts contributed to your HSA that exceed the IRS-determined maximums for that year. You must pay income tax for this amount as well as a 6% excise tax penalty. Even if an employer contribution caused the excess contribution, the employee bears the responsibility for the income and federal excise taxes.

To avoid paying the penalty, do the following:

- Withdraw the excess contributions by the due date of your tax return for the tax year during which you made the contributions (for example, by April 15, 2022, for contributions made in 2021).

- Withdraw not only the contributions, but also any income earned on the withdrawn contributions. Include the earnings in "other income" on your tax return.[25]

Note that even if you avoid the excise tax, you may still pay income tax on the excess contribution.

Testing period failures

If you used the full-contribution rule to make an entire year's contribution to your HSA but did not fulfill the testing period, you may pay a 10% penalty, plus income tax on the overage.

---

25   IRC §223(f)(3), IRS Notice 2004-2 Q&A 22

If, before the tax filing deadline for the previous year, you learn that you will not meet the testing period requirements, you can withdraw the excess contribution plus earnings, as described in the previous section.

Calculating penalties

If you lose your eligibility after the previous year's tax filing deadline, follow the steps in the "Testing period" section earlier in this chapter to calculate the amount of your over-contribution. To determine how much additional tax you will need to pay, download IRS Form 5329 from www.irs.gov and fill out the worksheet.

Summary

- You can make tax-deductible contributions to your HSA, whether you contribute pre-tax wages or after-tax money for which you later take an above-the-line deduction on your federal income tax form. Either way, the contributions you make do not count as taxable income.

- Anyone—you, your employer, your family, etc.—may contribute to your HSA. Keep in mind that all donations count towards the annual limit on how much you can contribute. (This limit changes nearly every year, with the family maximum usually twice the individual maximum.)

- If you exceed the annual contribution limit (even if your employer made the contribution that put you over the limit), you will—in most cases—pay a 6% excise tax as well as paying income tax on the overage.

- Enhance your savings by carefully planning contributions and monitoring your progress toward meeting your deductible.

- The full-contribution rule allows you to contribute the entire allowable amount to your HSA if you open it before the first day of the last month of the tax year—usually December 1. If you make the maximum contribution under the full-contribution rule, you must remain eligible until the last day of the next tax year (known as the testing period). If you lose eligibility during the testing period, you will pay income tax as well as a 10% excise tax on the overage.

- Qualifying life events—marriage, divorce, a new baby, stepchildren, adoption, changing or losing a job, disability, death—all present new coverage needs. Be sure to make the necessary enrollment changes as soon as the opportunity presents itself.

- In most cases, you must make your enrollment or coverage changes within 30 days of the life event.

- Having an HRA or FSA makes you ineligible to contribute to your HSA unless it's specifically designed to work with an HSA. HSA-qualified versions of those programs exist that do not disqualify you from opening or contributing to an HSA.

CHAPTER 7

Spending HSA Funds

Chapter overview

Under the law, HSA distributions are tax-free if used for qualified medical expenses incurred by the following people:

- You and your spouse (but not domestic partner)

- Any dependents you claim on your tax return

- Any person you might have claimed as a dependent on your taxes if the person had not filed a joint return or had a gross income of $4,300 or more.

- Even if you claim adult children (or others) as dependents on your taxes, they may pay qualified medical expenses from their own HSAs for their own dependents.[1]

Over the many years you own an HSA, you might experience life events that affect your eligibility to have an HSA, the amount you can contribute to your HSA, what kinds of distributions you can make from your HSA, and if you can have other kinds of health coverage besides the HSA-qualified HDHP that allows you to contribute to your HSA.

This chapter describes the kind of decisions you might need to make when you face a significant medical event or major life change such as job loss, marriage or divorce, childbirth or adoption, or disability.

---

1   IRC §223(d)(2)(A), IRS Notice 2008-59 Q&A 33, IRS Pub. 969)

Qualified medical expenses

Your HSA can be used for a wide variety of medical expenses, including those which are deducted from your individual tax return, if you are eligible. See Appendix C for a detailed list of qualified medical expenses.

If you use money from your HSA for non-medical purposes, you will add that amount to your gross income and also pay a 20% penalty on the amount.[2]

However, if the account holder (or other tax-qualified dependents) is over the age of 65, HSA funds may be used for non-qualified expenses without paying a penalty. Income taxes will still apply.[3]

Timing of expenses

Only expenses incurred after you establish your HSA qualify. You may not have funds dispersed for expenses incurred before you establish your HSA.[4] See Chapter 5 for more details about the date of establishment.

Qualified medical expenses

Appendix C has a detailed list of qualified medical expenses. In general, qualified medical expenses include:

- The costs of diagnosis, cure, mitigation, treatment or prevention of disease, and the costs for treatments affecting any part or function of the body.[5]

- Payments for legal medical services rendered by physicians, surgeons, dentists, and other medical practitioners, including the costs of equipment, supplies, and diagnostic devices needed for these medical services.

- Goods and services necessary to alleviate or prevent a physical or mental defect or illness—not including items or activities needed to improve general health, such as vitamins (unless prescribed) or a vacation (even if prescribed).

- Premiums for qualified long-term care insurance, COBRA premiums, and insurance premiums paid during periods of unemployment.

- Some other long-term care expenses, beyond premiums.

2   IRC §223(f)(4)(A)
3   IRC §223(f)(4)(B) and (C)
4   IRS Notice 2004-50 Q&A 39
5   IRC §213(d)

Services not covered under your health plan

You can also use your HSA balance to pay for healthcare not covered under your health plan, within the limits of qualified medical expenses. This includes many dental and vision expenses, as well as less common expenses, such as removing lead-based paint from your residence. Although these are HSA-qualified expenses, they do not count toward your deductible because health plans do not usually cover those types of expense. See Appendix C for more details.

Limited access

The trustee or custodian of your HSA has the legal right to limit or deny distributions under certain circumstances. For example, the trustee may prohibit distributions for amounts of less than $50 or might only allow a certain number of distributions per year.

If easy access to your account is important to you, clarify this issue when shopping for an HSA.

Insurance or health coverage premiums

Generally, you cannot use your HSA to pay medical insurance or health coverage premiums, but exceptions exist.[6]

Medicare premiums

Once you are 65 and eligible for Medicare, you can use your HSA to pay Medicare premiums (A, B, C, and D), out-of-pocket expenses that Medicare does not pay, and Medicare HMO premiums.

You cannot pay Medicare supplement insurance (Medigap) premiums with your HSA. Medigap insurance, sold by private companies, covers some remaining healthcare costs, such as copayments, coinsurance, and deductibles.

---

6   IRC §223(d)(2)(C); IRS Notice 2004-2 Q&A 27; IRS Notice 2005-59 Q&A 29

Premiums for employer-based coverage after 65

If you work beyond age 65, you can pay your share of premiums for employer-based coverage out of your HSA, but not if you already pay your share through pre-tax salary reductions.

Those over 65 who do not work can use an HSA to pay the share of premiums required for your employer-sponsored retiree healthcare coverage.

Premiums for the unemployed

You can also pay for healthcare coverage from your HSA while receiving unemployment compensation under federal or state law, including COBRA premiums.

Long-term care insurance

You may use your HSA to pay premiums for qualified long-term care insurance that meets criteria determined by federal law.[7]

Methods of payment from an HSA

The basic process of paying for care using an HSA is much the same as it is under other healthcare plans.

Traditional plan

In a traditional plan, you typically pay for care in one of two ways, depending on if the doctor or other provider participates in your plan's network.

In-network care

If the provider participates in your network, you typically present your healthcare plan membership card and pay the required copayment at the time of the visit. The provider files your claim with the insurance company and gets paid the contractually agreed or repriced amount. If coinsurance applies, then the provider bills you for the balance due.

7   IRS Publication 969

Out-of-network care

If the provider does not participate in your plan's network, you generally pay the entire bill at the time of the visit because an out-of-network provider does not usually submit the claim to your plan for you. Your insurance company will reimburse you for part of what you paid, depending on how much of your deductible has been met for the year.

HSA-qualified HDHP

With an HSA-qualified HDHP, the payment process at the doctor's office (or hospital, laboratory, or other facility) is similar. Typically, your health plan provider will pay the provider and then the provider will bill you for any balance for which you are responsible.

Your HSA administrator may supply you with an HSA debit card or checkbook. They may also provide an online bill pay service that lets you pay providers directly from your HSA for any balance for which you are responsible.

In-network care

For providers in your network (or for preventive care services), you may not have to pay anything at the time you receive care, depending on the structure of your plan. If the provider asks you to pay part of the bill at the time of your visit, try not to pay the entire bill because repricing often lowers the bill. Also, remember that under the PPACA, your health plan is required to cover preventive care without cost to you.

After you receive care, the provider generally submits your claim to your insurance company for repricing. The health plan pays its contractually agreed amount, which varies depending on if you have met your deductible for the year.

Depending on your healthcare plan, you can either pay your portion using your bank account or other form of payment and file for reimbursement from your HSA—or pay the amount directly out of your HSA using a debit card or online bill-pay system.

Out-of-network care

If your provider does not participate in your plan's network, you may need to pay at the time you receive care. As with in-network care, you can pay the expense using your bank account (or credit card) and file for reimbursement or pay the amount directly out of your HSA using your HSA debit card or online bill-pay system.

If you over-pay the provider from your HSA, you must re-deposit any reimbursement you may receive due to repricing or your health plan's payment into your HSA to avoid additional taxes.

Using healthcare wisely

Imagine you have just been told you need surgery. If you understand your HSA-qualified HDHP, you can focus on making the best choices for your long-term medical and financial well-being.

Conducting research

Spend time researching your condition, the treatment possibilities, and the risks and benefits of certain treatments. Use the internet, visit a library, and speak with friends and relatives who may have had a similar condition. Many HSA administrators and health plans offer powerful online tools that provide explanations, photographs, and videos of possible treatments.

Getting a second opinion

If you have been told you need surgery, get a second or third opinion because professionals often have different solutions to fix a health problem and most conditions can wait until you and your doctors understand your options.

Even if you have not met your HSA-qualified HDHP's annual deductible, understand your plan's requirements concerning surgery. Many plans require you get authorization for non-emergency surgery and some may require a second opinion before authorization is given. You can use your HSA to pay for any out-of-pocket expenses incurred to obtain a second opinion from any expert you choose whether or not that doctor is in your plan's network.

Following the rules of your HSA-qualified HDHP can cut waste, save money, and allow you to use your HSA funds when you need them most.

Choosing your doctor and hospital

Like other health plans, an HSA-qualified HDHP gives you the freedom to use either in-network or out-of-network providers. If you are facing a major medical event, such as surgery, explore the options in your network fully before checking out-of-network resources.

Whether or not your plan has separate out-of-pocket limits for in-network and out-of-network care will help you decide if you want to use a doctor or hospital in or out of your plan's network. If your plan has separate limits, you might pay thousands of dollars more for comparable care to that provided in your network. Additionally, in-network providers will typically accept deeper discounts for their services than out-of-network providers, which can also save you money.

If you have not yet accrued much money in your HSA, you may initially have to pay with after-tax dollars. Many hospitals and physicians will finance your debt and you can use future HSA contributions to make these payments, or to reimburse yourself if you pay the expenses with other funds. Balance this course of action against any interest charges that the hospital or physician may charge, because you cannot pay interest charges from your HSA.

If you are contemplating surgery, remember there will be many people involved in the procedure in addition to your principal surgeon. For example, choose an anesthesiologist in your plan's network to take full advantage of your benefits.

Ask your doctor which specialists will be involved in your surgery and where your doctor has operating privileges. Then, call the hospital and the other specialists and find out if they are part of your network. Your health plan can often provide this information by telephone or online. If the provider is not part of the network, they may be willing to give you a prompt-payment discount or honor your in-network pricing if you ask in advance.

The time you take to research these questions can save you a lot of money.

Obtaining authorizations and referrals

Make sure you know your plan's requirements concerning authorizations and referrals. Your plan may impose financial penalties if you do not get required referrals and authorizations, even for in-network providers. Penalties will not count toward meeting your out-of-pocket limit for the year. Choosing not to follow the plan's rules can cost you money.

Example: Negotiating discounts with an out-of-network provider

Serena is a 34-year-old metal worker who has been referred by her primary care physician to a surgeon for elective gallbladder removal due to pain and polyps.

The surgeon Serena has been referred to is not in her health plan's network. She feels comfortable with this surgeon and wants to use him anyway.

The surgeon's office explains that since Serena has an HSA and can pay promptly, they will offer a discounted fee, charging her only $50 more than a provider would charge in her network.

Serena then finds out that her out-of-network surgeon can perform surgery in both the in-network surgery center and an out-of-network hospital in her town.

Serena's surgeon agrees to schedule Serena's surgery at the in-network surgery center, because this will save her significant out-of-pocket expenses.

Serena is willing to pay a little extra money in surgeon fees to have the gallbladder removal performed by the surgeon of her choice.

Because she is informed and selective, Serena saves potentially thousands of dollars by having her surgery performed at the in-network surgery center.

Experiencing a medical emergency

Know your plan's rules about whom to call or visit in an emergency.

Generally, you or your representative (such as a family member) must communicate with your plan within 24 to 48 hours of the onset of an emergency. However, if you are initially taken to an out-of-network facility, you may not have to change hospitals until your condition stabilizes.

As in the case of surgery, however, treatment of an emergency is likely to be expensive and you should consider using in-network providers once the danger period has passed.

If your situation is not life-threatening, you may want to call the health plan's urgent care line or nursing hotline before seeking care (the number is generally on the back of your health plan card).

An urgent condition is one that needs treatment within 24 hours to prevent it from turning into a serious or life-threatening illness. Calling first can be especially important if you are out-of-town, as the urgent care line personnel may be able to direct you to an urgent care center or hospital near you that is part of your plan's network (remember, many plans are national in scope and have in-network providers all over the country).

Using an in-network provider will save you money and stretch your HSA dollars. If you are not sure whether your condition is urgent or an emergency, err on the side of caution: head for the emergency room first, and call later.

Losing eligibility

Even if you lose eligibility to contribute to your HSA, you can continue to spend the funds for qualified medical expenses.

Job changes

Job loss

If you lose your job, change jobs, have your working hours reduced, or your employer changes the plan it offers, you may lose HSA-qualified HDHP coverage, which would make you ineligible to contribute to an HSA.

Even if you lose eligibility to contribute to your HSA, you can still use the money in the account to pay for qualified medical expenses. You continue to own the account, even though you can no longer contribute to it. If you purchase an HSA-qualified HDHP in the future, you may resume contributions.

COBRA provides an important safety net when you lose your employer-sponsored medical coverage. Although the premiums can appear expensive, COBRA coverage protects you in a couple of ways:[8]

- Your qualified medical expenses continue to be covered.

- You are credited for payments toward your deductible made during the current year.

---

8   IRC §223(d)(2)(c)(1); IRS Notice 2004-2 Q&A 27, IRS Notice 2008-59 Q&A 32

A number of job changes can trigger COBRA eligibility, including quitting your job, getting laid off, retiring, or getting fired (other than for gross misconduct, which COBRA does not specifically define and might depend on specific facts and circumstances as well as your employer's determination). Generally, most reasons for involuntary termination, such as excessive absences or generally poor performance, do not amount to gross misconduct.

Having your work hours reduced may also trigger COBRA eligibility (unless your company provides health coverage for part-time employees). A strike by unionized employees can qualify as a reduction in hours.

If you choose COBRA coverage, you can use your HSA to pay COBRA premiums and can continue to contribute to your HSA.

New job

Many employers impose a waiting period before newly hired employees can enroll in health coverage. If you have a new job that imposes a waiting period and have either a self-only HSA-qualified HDHP or COBRA continuation coverage from your last job, you can continue to make HSA contributions during this waiting period.

If your new employer offers an HSA-qualified HDHP, look into transferring your old HSA over to the new one. You can make an unlimited number of direct trustee-to-trustee transfers.

Company changes

Employer bankruptcy

If your company closes or files for bankruptcy, it may no longer have a health plan and COBRA coverage may not be available.

If, however, another plan is offered through a successive employer, you may have COBRA rights through that employer. If you are offered COBRA coverage, you may use your HSA to pay those premiums. Or, if you purchase HSA-qualified coverage, you can also continue making contributions to your HSA.

If no COBRA coverage is available, you can use your HSA to pay for medical expenses or other coverage, including insurance premiums you might be able to buy while receiving unemployment compensation.

Company closure

If your employer is subject to COBRA and your plant or branch office closes but the rest of the company or a parent company remains in business, your employer must offer you COBRA coverage if you lose your job and health coverage as a result of the closure. You can use your HSA to pay those premiums.

Job loss related to company acquisition

If your company is sold and you lose your job, the buyer may be obliged to provide you with COBRA coverage. If COBRA coverage is available, you can use your HSA to pay those premiums.

Employer changes insurance plan

Termination of a health plan does not trigger COBRA eligibility. You can no longer contribute to an HSA if your HSA-qualified HDHP is terminated, but you can continue to use your HSA for medical expenses. You can also opt for another HSA-qualified plan or a non-HSA-qualified health plan if offered by your employer. However, if you choose a health plan that is not HSA-qualified, you cannot contribute to your HSA.

Other changes

Retirement before Medicare eligibility

Many people retire before age 65, the age for Medicare eligibility.

If you retire before age 65, you can use your HSA for a wide range of medical expenses. You can use it to pay COBRA premiums, premiums for long-term care insurance, or premiums for coverage you may buy on your own (if you are receiving unemployment compensation). You may also use your HSA balance to directly pay for qualified medical expenses.

If you retire from your job, accept a pension from your employer, and go to work for another employer, you cannot use your HSA to make any premium payments that your new employer may require unless you are at least age 65.

Medicare recipients should realize that Medigap insurance or Medicare Supplement coverage—private insurance that covers out-of-pocket costs not covered by Medicare—is not a qualified expense that can be paid with your HSA. Medigap is not the same thing as retiree health insurance; you buy a Medigap policy from a private insurer, while your employer provides retiree health insurance. If you have retiree health insurance, you will generally not need Medigap coverage.[9]

Medicare enrollment

Once you enroll in Medicare, you are no longer eligible to make HSA contributions. Remember, enrolling in SSI (the income portion of Social Security) automatically enrolls you in Medicare Part A and means you are no longer eligible to make HSA contributions.

Like early retirees, you can use the HSA to pay COBRA premiums, premiums for long-term care insurance, or non-COBRA premiums for coverage you buy on your own (if you are receiving unemployment compensation.) You can also use your HSA balance to pay qualified medical expenses directly.

If you remain employed after age 65, you can use your HSA to pay your share, if any, for employer-sponsored healthcare coverage as long as those amounts aren't already paid for by pre-tax salary reductions.

If your employer offers healthcare coverage to retirees or their survivors and requires a premium contribution from participating retirees or survivors, your HSA can be used to pay for that coverage as well.

You can also use your HSA to pay Medicare premiums once you reach age 65.

Personal bankruptcy

Because HSAs fall under laws governing savings accounts (and not those governing healthcare), most are not protected from creditors in the event of personal bankruptcy. This means that if creditors use the money in the HSA towards outstanding debits, the account holder is subject to income tax and the 20% penalty on the amount used for nonqualified distributions.

However, under the 2005 federal bankruptcy law, an individual debtor may deduct any reasonably necessary health insurance, disability insurance, and Health Savings Account expenses for the debtor, the spouse of the debtor, or the dependents of the debtor when determining his or her statement of monthly income.

---

9   IRS Notice 2004-2 Q&A 27

HSA as collateral[10]

Account beneficiaries (the owner) and HSA trustees and custodians cannot enter into a prohibited transaction with the HSA. A prohibited transaction is the sale, exchange, or lease of property; borrowing or lending money; furnishing goods, services, or facilities; or the transferring to or use by or for the benefit of the beneficiary of any assets contained in the account.

The beneficiary also may not pledge the assets of the HSA. Any amount used for such purposes is treated as a distribution and is included in the beneficiary's gross income because it is not used for medical expenses. A 20% excise tax penalty for such distributions applies.[11]

Disability

Since you do not need to work in order to make HSA contributions, there is no impact to your ability to make HSA contributions if you can continue to be covered by your employer's or another HSA-qualified HDHP plan after becoming disabled.

If you are covered by an HSA-qualified HDHP and qualify for short-term or long-term disability benefits under your employer-sponsored plan, nothing should change if your employer's healthcare coverage remains the same during the disability period.

However, because your HSA must be paired with an HSA-qualified HDHP, you will no longer be eligible to contribute to an HSA if you lose your employer-sponsored coverage because you can no longer work, unless you qualify for COBRA or can find an HSA-qualifying HDHP as an individual. You can use your HSA balance to make COBRA payments if you become eligible for COBRA coverage.

Note: If you must take a distribution from your HSA for non-medical expenses because you are disabled, the distribution will be subject to income tax but not to excise tax[12].

Social Security Disability Insurance

If you qualify for Social Security Disability Insurance (SSDI) benefits, everything changes. Qualifying for SSDI benefits is a separate process from qualifying for benefits under an employer-sponsored disability plan. By law, to qualify for SSDI benefits, you must be unable to do any substantial amount of work due to your health or your

---

10   IRC §223(e)(2), IRC §4975, IRS Notice 2004-50 Q&A 67
11   IRC §223(f)(4)(A)
12   IRC §223(f)(4)(B)

condition must have already lasted a year and be expected to last at least another year, or be expected to result in your death.[13]

Applicants have to be unable to do substantial work for at least five months before filing an application. Roughly half of SSDI applications are rejected. If you are awarded SSDI benefits, you become eligible for Medicare coverage two years later. Once you are covered by Medicare, you are no longer eligible to make HSA contributions because Medicare is considered disqualifying coverage.

You can continue to use your HSA both during the application process and after you are awarded benefits. Prior to being awarded SSDI benefits, you can use your HSA to pay COBRA premiums if eligible and can continue to make contributions as long as you continue to be covered by an HSA-qualified HDHP and no other disqualifying coverage.[14] You can also use your HSA for other medical expenses.

Death

When the account owner dies, any amount remaining in the HSA passes to the entity or individual named as the HSA's beneficiaries. If the owner's surviving spouse is the named beneficiary, the HSA becomes the HSA of the surviving spouse.[15]

An HSA is considered an individual account and as such, the spouse inheriting the HSA is considered the owner. The spouse can then use the HSA as any other HSA owner would. The surviving spouse is subject to income tax on amounts in the account only if not used for qualified medical expenses.

If the HSA passes to a person or persons other than a surviving spouse, then the HSA ceases to be an HSA, and the heir or heirs are required to include the fair market value of the HSA as gross income.[16] Fair market value is calculated as of the date of the account owner's death and is reduced by any payments made from the HSA on behalf of the decedent within one year of death.[17]

Choose a beneficiary when you set up your HSA. What happens to your HSA when you die depends on who you designate as the beneficiary. If your estate is the beneficiary, the value of your HSA is included on your final income tax return.

---

13   According to IRS Publication 524, "Substantial gainful activity is the performance of significant duties over a reasonable period of time while working for pay or profit, or in work generally done for pay or profit. Full-time work (or part-time work done at your employer's convenience) in a competitive work situation for at least the minimum wage conclusively shows that you're able to engage in substantial gainful activity."

14   IRC §223(d)(2)(c)(1)

15   IRC §223(f)(8)(A); IRS Notice 2004-2 Q&A 31

16   IRC §223(f)(8)(B)(i)

17   IRC §223(f)(8)(B)(ii)

Summary

- Research all options for using your HSA. Familiarize yourself with qualified medical expenses, investment options, and other rules and regulations in order to spend and save your money wisely.

- For the most accurate information about qualified medical expenses, see Title 26 Internal Revenue Code §213, which describes tax-deductible medical expenses (all of which are eligible) and §223(2)(A), which broadens coverage (for example, to include over-the-counter medication and other health-related costs such as removal of lead-based paint), but prohibits transportation costs and insurance premiums. The IRS provides two helpful publications that are updated every year. The first, Publication 502, lists eligible healthcare expenses that can be deducted on your taxes. This publication and Publication 969 provide helpful guidance in understanding how to most effectively and compliantly use your HSA. Appendix C provides a summary list of eligible expenses.

- In general, you cannot use your HSA to pay medical insurance premiums, but you can pay Medicare premiums from your HSA. Some other exceptions exist.

- Research your options before having surgery to minimize surprises.

- HSAs can help you with employment changes and transitions in and out of the workforce.

- Enrolling in Medicare puts an end to making contributions to your HSA. However, you can still use the funds you have built up in your HSA for a variety of healthcare expenses.

CHAPTER 8
Saving and Investing HSA Funds

Chapter overview

As you learn more about how your HSA-qualified health plan works and how to manage your HSA, you can stretch the dollars in your account to cover more healthcare needs or, better yet, to save more money, year over year, for future use.

By strategically contributing to your HSA and your other retirement accounts, you can reduce your tax burden and increase financial stability in your retirement years, especially for healthcare expenses you have in retirement.

Saving your HSA funds

Channeling premium savings to your HSA

A higher deductible generally means lower monthly premiums.

While it may seem intimidating to take on a high deductible, an HDHP may actually save you money over time. If you contribute all or some of what you save by paying lower premiums into your HSA, the balance in your account offsets your higher deductible. When you contribute more than you require for medical expenses in any given year, your account grows. Unlike use-it-or-lose-it funds, like FSA contributions, your HSA balance can grow every year.

As an example, car insurance with a $50 deductible has higher premiums than a policy with a $500 deductible. Much like you make decisions regarding your car insurance costs, you make similar decisions regarding your health plan coverage. Decide whether you want to pay higher upfront costs and save for unexpected costs, or if you prefer the higher premium costs with less up-front exposure. Doing the math usually points to a lower premium and the ability to set aside money for those unexpected costs that may or may not occur.

Considering coinsurance and copayments

Coinsurance and copayment levels can inversely affect your premium price—the higher your share of costs, the lower the premium price.

Likewise, you will probably pay a higher premium for a health plan that covers 100% of costs (your plan pays 100% after the deductible) than for an 80/20 coinsurance plan (the plan pays 80% and you pay 20% until you meet your out-of-pocket maximum).

The amounts of coinsurance and copayments also affect how much you may need to pay out of your HSA (or out of pocket) after you meet your deductible.

Keep in mind that most coinsurance levels can also vary for in- and out-of-pocket network care.

Using an HSA with an HRA or FSA

In general, having an HSA requires you to have coverage under an HSA-qualified HDHP and have no other disqualifying coverage. As examples, some employers offer a

Health Reimbursement Arrangement (HRA) or Health Flexible Spending Account (FSA) that provide coverage before the deductible is satisfied and thus disqualify you from opening or contributing to an HSA. But some employers offer HSA-qualified HRAs or FSAs to cover the gap between the deductible and out-of-pocket maximum for HSA owners. These plans are discussed more fully in Chapter 4. Study the requirements for these benefits, keep accurate records of your expenses, and watch the calendar— many people neglect to submit reimbursement requests to their employers before the end-of-year submission deadlines for FSAs and HRAs.

If you have an LPFSA in conjunction with your HSA, talk to your dentist and vision services providers during open enrollment to get an estimate of the dental and vision care you will need, then make an election for an LPFSA contribution to cover that amount. Make sure you do not over-contribute to the LPFSA because you can lose any unspent money at the end of the year (unless your employer's plan allows a grace period or carryover provision, which is also discussed in more detail in Chapter 4.) Using an HSA-qualified FSA or HRA for your dental and vision expenses instead of your HSA lets you stretch your HSA balance.

These HSA-qualified FSAs make the most sense for people who contribute the annual maximum to their HSA. Always "top off" your HSA before contributing to your HSA-qualified FSA. Although you can use HSA dollars for dental and vision, you can maximize your savings by contributing to both accounts and first spending the funds from your HSA-qualified FSA.

Again, if you have an HSA, you may not contribute to a general Health FSA, but you may use the HSA-qualified version of an FSA or HRA, or both.

2021 Contribution Limits

	Individual	Family	Over-55	Use-or-Lose
HSA	$3,600	$7,200	$1,000	No
HSA-qualified FSA	$2,750	$2,750	$0	Sometimes; depends on employer design
HSA-qualified HRA	Employer-funded			Depends on employer design

Using gap coverage

The HSA law allows you to use certain other types of insurance with your HSA-qualified HDHP that can help offset the risk that comes with a higher deductible and doesn't disqualify you from making HSA contributions.[1]

These policies include homeowner's insurance, automobile insurance, dental and vision care plans, accidental injury insurance, workers' compensation benefits, hospital indemnity plans (which pay a fixed amount per day of hospitalization), and specific disease policies that pay a fixed amount for a designated disease.

The permitted plans help preserve your HSA balance and protect you from out-of-pocket expenses[2].

Determining how much to contribute

Try to contribute as much money to your HSA as the law (and your family budget) allows, because HSAs have the best tax benefits of any savings accounts, including traditional IRAs, 401(k)s, and Roth IRAs.

Among other insurance plans and retirement accounts, only an HSA lets you make tax-deductible contributions, enjoy tax-free growth through interest or investments, and spend the money on qualified medical expenses and products without paying federal income tax.

Unlike most other medical spending accounts such as FSAs or HRAs, the money in your HSA is yours to keep. You may use your HSA to pay non-health related costs when you reach 65, paying only income tax, but no penalties.[3]

If you have a tight budget and can't fully fund your HSA, remember that most plans allow you to make contributions beyond the end of the year (until the tax filing deadline) and still receive tax benefits.

Funding strategies for HSAs and 401(k)s

Many employers offer both 401(k)s for retirement security and HSAs for healthcare security now and into retirement. Employees who can contribute to both of these

---

1   IRC §223 (c) (3)
2   IRC §223(c)(3)(C)
3   After age 65, if you withdraw funds for any purpose other than qualified medical expenses, you will be subject to income taxes. Funds withdrawn for qualified medical expenses will remain tax-free.

accounts should consider the unique triple-tax advantage of the HSA when they decide how to allocate contributions between the benefits. Maximize your saving potential by funding your accounts in such a way that you receive the full benefits of both.

- Remember that an HSA provides tax-free reimbursement for any money that you will need to spend on healthcare now and in your future and an HSA can be used after the age of 65 for non-healthcare spending without penalty. At that time, it will be subject to the same tax consequences as traditional IRAs and 401(k)s/403(b)s.

- Determine if your employer contributes to either your HSA or other retirement accounts, the level of this contribution, and if a match is required to obtain the employer funding. It is usually a good idea to make sure you get your full employer contribution in either of the accounts.

- Think about the total amount of money that you have in your budget to contribute collectively to ALL of your retirement accounts.

Considering these factors, **first** contribute enough money to your HSA and other retirement accounts to capture the maximum of your employer's matching funds. **Then** contribute to your HSA up to the allowable annual maximum contribution, including catch-up contributions if they are available to you. **Finally**, if you are able to contribute more money, contribute funds to your 401(k) up to the annual maximum.

Applying this logic, consider funding your accounts in the following order to maximize your income and your tax benefits.[4] As always, discuss your funding strategy with your accountant or other tax professional.

1. Ensure you have a personal emergency reserve (about three months of living expenses).

2. Contribute enough in your HSA to take full advantage of employer matching contributions, then do the same for your defined contribution plan, such as a 401(k).

3. Pay down higher-interest loans, such as credit card debt and student loans.

4. After you have optimized employer matching, fund your HSA to the allowable annual maximum, then fully fund your 401(k) or other defined contribution plan.

5. Pay down lower interest loans, such as student loans with interest less than 5.75%.

---

4   According to Sharon Carson, Executive Director, JP Morgan (6/9/21 EBRI webinar, "Saving for Health Care in Retirement: How HSAs and 401(k)s Fit Together")

6. Contribute to a traditional IRA or Roth IRA if eligible.

This strategy allows you to fully benefit from employer matching funds while minimizing your taxable income. To enhance your savings even more, consider paying your medical expenses out of pocket, if you can afford to.

Using payroll deductions

If you foresee a large medical expense during the year, try to increase your payroll deduction in anticipation or fully fund your HSA at the beginning of the year, particularly if you expect to retain HSA-qualified HDHP coverage for the entire year.

Example: Funding an HSA early in the year

The Kim family is expecting their second child in July and their HSA-qualified HDHP plan year began on January 1, 2021.

They have family coverage with a $5,000 deductible and no embedded deductible. Their plan has maternity coverage and no coinsurance once they meet their deductible.

Expecting out-of-pocket expenses in July associated with the birth of their child, they increase their HSA contributions to $800 per month, so that by July 1, they will have contributed $4,800 in their HSA for the year.

For the 2021 tax year, the Kims can contribute up to $7,200 to their account, meaning they can still contribute $2,400 over the next six months if they remain eligible to contribute to the HSA for the entire year.

By the time they receive bills for the birth, they will have enough money in their HSA to satisfy their entire $5,000 deductible. Costs exceeding $5,000 will be fully paid by their HSA-qualified health plan for in-network expenses.

Shopping carefully

There are many opportunities to compare costs and shop for bargains on prescriptions and medical supplies, both through your health plan and by doing a little research on the internet. Don't forget there are several good websites that rate hospitals and compare treatment costs. Your HSA administrator may provide links for cost comparison tools and websites on your HSA member portal.

You might also consider home-use alternatives to medications or supplies.

Examples

As you become familiar with the covered benefits, deductibles, contributions, and out-of-pocket expenses associated with your HSA-qualified HDHP, you can use your HSA more effectively.

The following examples and real-life scenarios show how HSAs can help decrease health coverage premiums and build good healthcare consumer skills. These studies illustrate how to get the most out of your HSA by:

- Understanding and selecting the best HSA-qualified HDHP design for your situation

- Determining the right amount of money to contribute to your HSA

So that you can easily make side-by-side comparisons, the employee contributes no money to their HSA in each of the examples below.

Testimonial: Finding healthcare bargains

Holly, age 35, a married mother of four recently received a diagnosis of insulin-dependent diabetes.

Holly's husband recently left a job that offered health benefits through a low deductible, traditional plan. His new employer offers an HSA-qualified HDHP.

In Holly's own words:

In a health insurance plan with a consistent copayment of $10, I never had a reason to ask questions about the costs of services. I just paid the copayment and felt grateful to have our health plan pay the rest—or so I thought.

Under my previous health plan, the pharmacy simply filled my prescriptions for insulin and supplies, and I didn't see any need to look for more cost-effective prices. I was happy to pay my $35 copayment for insulin.

When introduced to Health Savings Accounts, I was worried that I wouldn't get the same benefits. I learned, though, that not only did I receive comparable care, I also learned to be a careful shopper and save money.

I began to ask questions about such things as lab work, blood tests, and examinations. I learned how to save money by switching to generic drugs and buying a less expensive blood glucose monitor and test strips. I found out that the typical blood work done at my doctor's office costs anywhere from $55 to $70.

I found out that I could buy my own hemoglobin A1C test at my pharmacy for about $24. I did the test at home and called my doctor with the results. I also learned to watch for coupons and rebates.

I've become more educated and I research healthcare issues for myself and for my children. For most issues, before taking them to the doctor or to the urgent care, I go online to learn what I can about their symptoms and possible treatments.

I've discovered that by controlling my own medical dollars, I'm more conscientious about what I'm doing and spending, and we have saved a lot of money. We've contributed those savings to our HSA and are starting to build a reserve for any unexpected healthcare costs we'll have—and with our active family, we're sure to have some!

Case Study 1: Chronic illness

Clark and Alexis, a middle-aged married couple, begin to need care for chronic conditions. During his employer's open enrollment period for 2022 benefits, Clark uses his and Alexis' medical history from 2021 to compare benefit options.

In 2021, Clark and Alexis took advantage of free preventive care screenings through their health plan. They also took medications for some mild chronic illnesses and had only one urgent care visit during the year.

	Clark	Alexis
Age	58	57
Health	High cholesterol	Type 1 diabetes
Medications	Lipitor®, 10 mg daily	Insulin, daily
Healthcare Utilization	Regular doctor and preventive visits. 1 urgent care visit for cut hand.	Regular doctor and preventive visits

To compare plans, Clark totals the premiums, medical expenses, and employer contributions to the HSA.

Even though he does not typically meet the relatively high HSA-qualified HDHP plan deductible and had to pay for healthcare expenses out of his HSA (and out of his own pocket after depleting the HSA), he still pays $1,303 less under the HSA-qualified HDHP.

	PPO plan		HDHP/HSA plan	
Money in				
Employer HSA contributions		$0	$125 x 12 months	$1,500
Money out				
Employee contribution to healthcare premiums[5]	$501.42 x 12 months	$6,017	$404.33 x 12 months	$4,852
Total provider visits	Copays	$115	Paid from HSA	$895
Total prescriptions	Copays	$140	Paid from HSA	$722
Money out subtotal		$6,272		$6,469
Less the HSA employer contribution		$0		-$1,500
Total money out		$6,272		$4,969
Difference in out-of-pocket expenditures				$1,303 savings
HSA balance remaining		$0		$0

5   Kaiser Family Foundation 2020 Employer Health Benefits Survey

Case Study 2: Excellent health

Li knows the importance of health insurance and good habits. She watches what she eats and gets enough exercise and sleep. She has a relatively low income and watches her budget carefully.

Li	
Age	35
Health	Excellent
Medications	One generic prescription for strep
Healthcare utilization	Two doctor visits: Annual checkup Strep throat

Like Clark, Li compares her two plan options using her expenses from 2021. Because she worries about the high deductible in the HSA-qualified HDHP, she finds the $0 deductible in the PPO very attractive. Even though she enjoys good health, she does not think she can afford unanticipated medical expenses, because she largely lives paycheck to paycheck.

She also notices that the out-of-pocket maximum for the HSA-qualified HDHP is $3,000, compared to the $2,000 from the PPO plan.

Her employer contributes $750 to her HSA, but she does not see much of an impact from that at first. Her co-worker encourages her to do the math.

Premiums and contributions

	PPO plan		HDHP/HSA plan	
Deductible		$0		$1,500
Out-of-pocket maximum		$2,000		$3,000
Annual premium contributions	$85 x 12 months	$1,020	$25 x 12 months	$300
Employer HSA contributions		N/A	$62.50 x 12 months	$750
Employee HSA contributions		N/A	$0 x 12 = $0	$0

Both of Li's insurance plans cover her annual checkup as a preventive benefit.

Provider visits

	PPO plan		HDHP/HSA plan	
Annual preventive exam	100% covered	$0	100% covered	$0
$100 doctor visit	$15 copay	$15	Pays from HSA	$100
Total office visit costs		$15		$100

Li purchased only one prescription in 2021: an antibiotic (generic instead of name brand) to treat strep throat.

Prescriptions

	PPO plan		HDHP/HSA plan
$25 generic	$10 copay	$10	$25.00
Total prescriptions		$10	$25.00

Everything comes into perspective when Li compares money in and money out. Between the low premium and her employer's contribution to her HSA, she saves money with an HSA-qualified HDHP.

Though worried about the high deductible and high out-of-pocket maximum, she actually finishes the year with a positive balance in her HSA (more than $600). Even with a $0 deductible, she would have paid at least $700 more with the PPO plan compared to the HSA-qualified plan when she factors in monthly premiums and copay costs.

	PPO plan		HDHP/HSA plan	
Money in				
Employer HSA contributions		$0	$62.50 x 12 months	$750
Money out				
Annual premium contributions	$85 x 12 months	$1,020	$25 x 12 months	$300
Total office visit costs	Copays	$15	Paid from HSA	$100
Total prescriptions	Copays	$10	Paid from HSA	$25
Total money out		$1,045		$425
Money out: PPO vs. HDHP/HSA			Savings	$620
HSA balance remaining		$0		$625

Case Study 3: Accidental injury

The Fishers have two children. Derek works for an electrical contractor and Lauren works at a local university. Lauren has better benefits, so she opts for family coverage from her employer.

They have two very active boys. One was injured in a bicycle accident in 2021. They have no reason to believe that the boys will become any less adventurous in 2022.

	Derek	Lauren	Children
Age	38	36	6 and 10
Health	Excellent	Excellent	One child required surgery
Medications	None	None	None
Healthcare utilization	Regular doctor and preventive visits	Regular doctor and preventive visits	Regular doctor and preventive visits, one ER visit, surgery, and 3-day stay for injury

Lauren compares her two 2022 plan options using the family's 2021 medical expenses as a guide. There is a PPO plan with a relatively low deductible and out-of-pocket maximum. For 2022, her employer introduced an HSA-qualified plan that has a much higher deductible and out-of-pocket limit, but no employee contribution. The company also makes a contribution to the employee's HSA.

Premiums and contributions

	PPO plan		HDHP/HSA plan	
Deductible		$250		$3,000
Maximum out-of-pocket limit		$2,500		$5,000
Coinsurance		20%		20%
Annual premium contributions	$400 x 12 months	$4,800	$0 x 12 months	$0
Employer HSA contributions		$0	$150 x 12 months	$1,800
Employee HSA contributions		N/A	$0 x 12 = $0	$0

The hospital expenses for the surgery far exceed the out-of-pocket maximum for both plans, so she only uses the out-of-pocket amounts to compare the actual costs of each plan.

Provider visits

	PPO plan		HDHP/HSA plan	
Two annual preventive exams	Preventive 100% covered	$0	Preventive 100% covered	$0
Emergency room, surgery, labs, prescriptions for bicycle accident	All expenses above out-of-pocket maximum paid 100% by health plan	$19,735	All expenses above out-of-pocket max. paid 100% by health plan	$19,735
Out-of-pocket maximum	Entire amount paid out-of-pocket	$2,500	$1,800 from HSA, $3,200 out of pocket	$5,000

When Lauren compares money in versus money out, she sees that the HSA-qualified HDHP option provided greater protection against out-of-pocket expenses.

	PPO plan		HDHP/HSA plan	
Money in				
Employer HSA contributions		$0	$150 x 12 months	$1,800
Money out				
Annual premiums	$400 x 12 months	$4,800	$0 x 12 months	$0
Provider costs		$2,500		$5,000
Money out subtotal		$7,300		$5,000
Less the HSA employer contribution		$0		$1,800
Total money out		$7,300		$3,200
Difference between PPO and HDHP/HSA money out				$4,100 savings
HSA balance remaining		$0		$0

With this plan design, Lauren saves $4,100 by choosing the HDHP/HSA plan, even with a large, unforeseen expense. She can save even more if she makes additional pre-tax contributions to her HSA.

Minimize spending, maximize savings

You can increase the balance in your HSA by both reducing expenditures and by increasing account earnings.

Retail pricing

Many providers, both in-and out-of-network, are unfamiliar with HSA-qualified HDHPs and will try to charge retail price when you receive services. Contact your HSA provider or health plan about how to obtain the best pricing when you visit your doctor.

Early HSA contributions

The law governing HSAs provides you and your employer with flexibility in funding your HSA. You or your employer can make contributions to the HSA on any schedule that you find convenient, as long as the total contributions made to your account in a given year do not exceed the annual maximum contribution limits.

Because you can never lose funds in your HSA, you do not risk forfeiting unspent dollars.

If you have a bill that exceeds your balance, you can pay the bill using other resources, then file for reimbursement from your HSA once your balance has grown sufficiently. Your HSA trustee will provide you with what you need in order to request reimbursements.

Return duplicate reimbursements to your HSA

If you pay directly from your HSA and then receive reimbursement from the health plan for the same claim or a refund from the provider due to discounted rates, return the reimbursed amount to the HSA administrator. If you do not return the duplicate reimbursement, you will have to pay a penalty to the IRS. This also applies to any refunds you receive from health providers for over-payment.

Mistaken distributions from an HSA can be repaid before the tax filing deadline without penalty, provided your HSA's trustee permits it, and you can provide "convincing evidence" that the amounts were distributed from an HSA because of a mistake.[6]

---

6   IRS Notice 2004-50 Q&A 37

Investing your HSA funds[7]

If you make your maximum annual contributions, manage your funds carefully, and look for ways to get the best value (for example, by comparing prescription prices at different pharmacies and using in-network providers), the money in your HSA will grow and earn interest over the years.

Investing the money in your HSA can increase the earning potential of your account, but also increases your risk. When your account balance reaches the minimum required by your HSA administrator (usually $1,000 or $2,000), you can invest any money over that threshold in HSA-qualified investment funds.

Investment options usually include mutual funds, stocks, and other investments. Most HSA administrators provide a website for you to set up investments and make trades.

You will not pay the federal tax on the increase in value in these investments, provided you spend the money on qualified medical expenses.

Investment choices

You can invest your HSA funds in the same investments approved for IRAs: bank accounts, annuities, certificates of deposit (CDs), stocks, mutual funds, and bonds. You cannot invest in life insurance contracts, collectibles (art, antiques, etc.), nor can you co-mingle HSA assets with other property, except in a common trust or investment fund.[8]

Earnings on money invested from your HSA accrue tax-free; however, all investments carry risk.

Investments made available to HSA holders are subject to risk, including the possible loss of the principal invested, and are not FDIC- or NCUA-insured. Investing may not be suitable for everyone and HSA holders making investments should review the applicable fund's prospectus. Investment options and thresholds may vary and are subject to change. Consult your advisor or the IRS with any questions regarding investing or filing your tax return.

---

7   IRS Notice 2004-50 Q&A 65
8   See IRC §408(m)

Paying qualified expenses from your invested HSA funds

If you have a large medical expense, you can move money out of your investments back into your HSA with no tax penalties and without affecting your yearly contribution maximum. This is because the IRS views this transfer as a dispersal, not a contribution.

If you choose an HSA administrator that offers no trading fees, you may also be able to make trades and maintain your investment account with no extra fees.

Other retirement savings accounts

Several other types of retirement savings account exist, including employer-sponsored plans funded through payroll deductions. You probably already use one of the most common retirement savings accounts to save for retirement, such as a 401(k) or IRA.

The following section provides a general overview of various types of accounts: IRA, Roth IRA, 401(k), 403(b), and Roth 401(k)s. If you want to learn more about these, or any other types of retirement plans such as Simple IRAs and SEP IRAs, talk to a tax advisor or certified financial planner (CFP), or consult a book written specifically about these types of retirement accounts.

A defined contribution (DC) plan, like a 401(k) or 403(b) allows employees to contribute pre-tax earnings towards retirement. Sometimes an employer will match a portion of employee contributions as an added benefit. These plans place restrictions that control when and how each employee can withdraw from these accounts without penalties.

- Defined contribution (DC) retirement plans allow employees to invest pre-tax dollars in the capital markets where they can grow tax-deferred until retirement.

- 401(k) and 403(b) are two popular defined contribution plans commonly used by companies and organizations to encourage employees to save for retirement.

- DC plans can be contrasted with defined benefit (DB) pensions, in which retirement income is guaranteed by an employer. With a DC plan, there are no guarantees and participation is both voluntary and self-directed.

In contrast to a defined contribution plan, a defined benefit plan, known also as a pension plan or a qualified benefit plan, provides guaranteed retirement benefits based on a formula that includes length of employment and salary history.

Traditional IRAs

An individual retirement account (IRA) allows you to make tax-deductible contributions to the account, reducing your taxable income. The amount of your tax deduction depends on your income and whether you have an employer-sponsored retirement account.

IRAs allow individuals to avoid taxes on contributions as well as on fund growth, such as interest, capital gains, and dividend income. With a traditional IRA, you pay taxes only when you withdraw the money. You can begin making withdrawals without penalty, paying ordinary income taxes on distributions, at age 59½. If you withdraw money before then, you will pay a 10% penalty in addition to ordinary income taxes.

Contribution limits to your IRA depend on your tax filing status as well as on your income and age. Consult a tax professional or a financial advisor to determine how much you can contribute to an IRA. For 2021, the maximum IRA contribution amount (per person) is $6,000 each year ($7,000 if you are 50 or older). After age 70½, you can no longer contribute to a traditional IRA.

When you reach 70 ½, you must take required minimum distributions (RMDs)— recalculated every year, based on your life expectancy. Failing to make an RMD is an expensive mistake that could lead to a 50% penalty plus taxes owed on the missed distribution.

Roth IRAs

The Roth IRA (named for Senator William Roth who helped establish the account in 1997) has many similarities to a traditional IRA, but differs in when you pay taxes.

You generally fund a traditional IRA with pre-tax dollars; with a Roth IRA, you use after-tax dollars, meaning contributions are not tax-deductible. However, once you begin withdrawing funds from the account, all distributions (including interest or earnings) are tax-free if the distribution comes at least five years after you established the account and at least one of the following applies:

- You are at least 59½ when the distribution occurs.

- You will use the funds to purchase (or build or rebuild) a first home for you or a qualified family member. A limit of $10,000 for this distribution is strictly enforced by the IRS.

- You become disabled.

- You die and your estate distributes the money in your Roth IRA.

Failure to comply with these rules could lead to the distribution being subject to income tax as well as a 10% penalty.

Unlike traditional IRAs, you can contribute to a Roth IRA after age 70½ and rules about required minimum distributions (RMDs) do not apply.

Contribution limits to Roth IRAs are the same as those for traditional IRAs.

401(k)s and 403(b)s

A 401(k) is the most common employer-sponsored retirement plan used today. Non-profit and public institutions such as schools, charities, and hospitals provide the nearly identical 403(b). Both have the same contribution limits and age requirements, but some minor differences exist. For example, 403(b)s need not apply nondiscrimination testing, which prevents highly compensated employees from benefitting disproportionately.

Both 401(k) and 403(b) accounts allow you and your employer to make contributions from your wages to an account specifically designed for retirement. Although you do not usually pay income tax on these contributions, you will pay tax when you withdraw the funds.

Similar to IRAs, your maximum contribution limit depends on your age and income level as well as other factors. In 2021, an employee may contribute up to $19,500 each year to their 401(k) or 403(b), with a $6,500 catch-up contribution allowed for those over 50. Employers can also contribute up to $37,500 to an employee's 401(k) depending on each employee's individual circumstances. The combined employee and employer contributions must not exceed $58,000 in 2021. A tax advisor or financial planner can help you calculate your maximum contribution limit based on your specific circumstances.

The IRS generally announces next year's 401(k) and 403(b) contribution limits (which tend to increase by about $500 every two or three years) in October.

The IRS limits how and when you can withdraw funds from your 401(k) or 403(b). Taking funds from the account too early can lead to significant tax penalties. Required annual minimum distributions also apply based on your age, retirement date, and other factors. For a side-by-side comparison of these accounts, see the following table.

	Traditional 401(k)	Roth 401(k)	Roth IRA	Traditional IRA
Origin		Since 2001	Since 1997	Since 1974
Overarching purpose	Employer-sponsored retirement savings	Hybrid of traditional 401(k) and Roth IRA	Vehicle for tax-free retirement withdrawals	Tax-advantaged retirement savings
Advantage	Highest tax advantage and contribution limit	Higher contribution limits vs. Roth IRA	Allows investment to grow longer	For people with no 401(k)
RMD[9]	After age 72	After age 72	No	After age 72
Income limit	No	No	Yes: $140K/$208K individual/ married couple in 2021	Yes: $76K/$104K individual/ married for tax advantage in 2021
Eligible contributors	Employer may contribute	Employer may contribute, with tax implications	Self only	Self only
Contribution limit	$19,500	$19,500	$6,000	$6,000
Catch-up	$6,500 if over 50	$6,500 if over 50	$1,000 if over 50	$1,000 if over 50
Tax advantage	Tax-free contributions	Tax-free distributions	Tax-free distributions. Eligible for tax saver's credit.	Tax-free contributions, depending on income and 401(k). Eligible for tax saver's credit.

---

9 Not required if still working and not a 5% owner of the company sponsoring the plan

	Traditional 401(k)	Roth 401(k)	Roth IRA	Traditional IRA
Distributions	Penalty for distributions before age 59 ½	Penalty for distributions before age 59 ½	Penalty to withdraw earnings before 59 ½ (with some exceptions)	Penalty to withdraw contributions or earnings before 59 ½ (with some exceptions)
Inheritance	Becomes part of taxable estate	May be tax free five years after deposit	May be tax free five years after deposit	Becomes part of taxable estate
Account compatibility	Can contribute to both Roth 401(k) and traditional 401(k), but contribution limit applies to both together		Can contribute to both Roth IRA and traditional IRA, but $6K + $1K limit applies to both together	
	Contribute to 401(k) and Roth IRA, if qualified, for maximum tax savings		Contribute to Roth IRA and 401(k) for maximum tax savings	

Summary

Employ various strategies to reduce your overall medical costs.

- Before selecting from among your available health plans, analyze your options by reviewing last year's healthcare costs against the options you have available, taking into account insurance premiums, employer contributions, tax liability, copay and coinsurance, deductibles, and out-of-pocket maximums.

- To maximize your tax benefit and help your savings grow as quickly as possible, consider the following strategy:

  1. Ensure you have a personal emergency reserve (about three months of living expenses).

  2. Contribute enough to your HSA to receive any contributions your employer may offer. Then, do the same for your 401(k).

  3. Pay down higher-interest loans, such as credit card debt and student loans.

  4. After you have paid enough into your HSA and 401(k) to receive free employer money, fund your HSA to the allowable annual maximum, then fully fund your 401(k).

  5. Pay down lower interest loans, such as student loans with interest less than 5.75%.

  6. Contribute to a Traditional IRA or Roth IRA.

  7. When your HSA funds have accrued sufficiently, begin to invest them— understanding that you trade higher risk for the potential of higher returns.

CHAPTER 9
Paperwork, Recordkeeping, Taxes

Chapter overview

You own the funds in your HSA, so treat your HSA (and HSA-related records) as you would your other financial accounts, including retirement accounts, investment and savings accounts, and credit cards. Check your statement each month and make sure you understand the charges to your account; if you don't, seek immediate explanation.

Set up an intuitive, easy-to-use filing system and keep accurate, well-organized records—not only to request reimbursement or calculate tax deductions, but also to prove the deductions claimed on your tax return if audited by the IRS.

Disputes or questions about billing and payments can arise even a year or two after a procedure or office visit. To reduce the stress associated with this, keep records in a way that allows you to easily reconstruct exactly how you spent your money.

Processing paperwork

You may find keeping track of HSA expenses, contributions, and earnings similar to sorting expenses you deduct on your income tax but using different categories.

Submitting expenses

Submitting expenses to your HSA-qualified HDHP

If your provider participates in your plan's network, they should submit your claim to your insurance plan. If not, you may have to file the claim yourself, for accurate tracking of your deductible and out-of-pocket limit. The plan should supply you with a form for filing claims, but many providers include enough information on the statement you receive before you leave the office that you can use the statement itself to file your claim. Remember: always keep copies of your statements in case of a dispute.

Requesting distributions from the HSA

Some HSA administrators provide a debit card or checkbook to pay HSA-eligible expenses directly from your HSA. You can also pay for qualified medical expenses from your personal account or credit card and then submit expenses for reimbursement from your HSA. Some HSA administrators make provisions for account holders to transfer funds electronically from their HSA to their personal account.

Regardless of how you get reimbursed, you can only be reimbursed for the expenses you incurred after your HSA was established[1]. See Chapter 3 for more details.

Unlike your health plan, an FSA, or HRA, your trustee or custodian does not determine if the distributions qualify as reimbursable medical expenses, so you must maintain proper records to prove your claims—especially if you need to pay with personal funds and seek reimbursement.

---

1   IRS Notice 2004-50 Q&A 39

Submitting expenses to another plan, such as an FSA or HRA

If you had an FSA in the past and your employer converts to an HSA-qualified HDHP with an HSA-qualified FSA or HRA, you will find the submission process very similar. You submitted expenses to your FSA or HRA administrator by providing an explanation of benefits form (see description below) or itemized receipt; your FSA or HRA will work in much the same way.

Reviewing insurance-related paperwork

Invoices and point-of-sale receipts

As of January 1, 2020, over-the-counter (OTC) medications no longer require a doctor's prescription to be considered a qualified medical expense. You can also purchase other items with your HSA, such as diabetic supplies, canes, reading glasses, and bandages (see Appendix C).

All receipts and invoices should have as much detail about the goods or services provided as possible, including date, item, service description, vendor, etc.

Explanation of benefits (EOB)

Your health plan periodically provides an EOB, a summary of charges and payment responsibilities. It shows how much the provider originally charged, how much your health plan paid the provider, and the contracted discounts to which your providers have agreed.

The EOB also shows your financial responsibility, summarizes the cost of the services provided during the doctor's visit, and updates you on your progress toward meeting the plan deductible.

Finally, the EOB explains the participant's right to dispute any statements made in the EOB.

HSA statements

Your HSA administrator will provide a periodic statement containing the following details concerning your account:

- Your contributions

- Contributions your employer made on your behalf

- Payments made to providers from your HSA

- Investment and interest earnings accrued

- Fees

Organize and save these statements the same way you do for other financial accounts, possibly even in the same place.

If you treat your HSA as a long-term savings vehicle, you can accumulate funds over a considerable period of time and may claim reimbursement from your account many years after you incur an eligible expenses. Because you might need to produce records about account transactions long after they occurred, keep all receipts and statements for at least three years after you receive reimbursement. (Tax audits usually occur within three years, though they can sometimes take as long as six years to occur.)

Sample of explanation of benefits

THIS IS NOT A BILL
(Please keep this form for your records)

EXPLANATION OF BENEFITS (EOB)

Carolyn Harper
82 Smith Street
Webster, IL 62372

Date: **March 12, 2022**
Benefit plan number: **XYZ00000000A**
Page number: **1 of 1**

Participant: **Caroline Harper**
Patient: **Caroline Harper**
Relationship: **Subscriber**

Member services
Local: **000.000.0000**
National: **800.000.0000**

Payment Summary					
Patient/claim no.	Paid to	Total charges	Covered amount	Previously processed	Patient responsibility
Caroline H 1234567890		$135.00	$60.00	$0.00	$75.00

Subscriber's responsibility: $75.00
Does not reflect any payments you may
have made to the provider.

Year-to-date cost sharing status: 2022

Applied to $3,000 per member deductible:
Caroline H. $75.00
$75.00 has accumulated toward deductible maximum.

Sample of periodic HSA statement

Caroline Harper
82 Smith Street
Webster, IL 62372

Account statement
Account number: **123456**
Period: **06/01/2018 to 06/30/2022**
Statement print date: **07/01/2022**

Date	Description of transaction	Deposit (or withdrawal)	Account balance
		Beginning balance	$ 8,803.98
06/02/2022	Employer contribution (Tax year: 2022)	$83.33	$8,887.31
06/02/2022	Employee contribution (Tax year: 2022)	$89.58	$8,976.89
06/03/2022	Payment for claim 219325-0142	($15.00)	$8,961.89
06/15/2022	Employee contribution (Tax year: 2022)	$89.58	$9,051.47
06/15/2022	Employer contribution (Tax year: 2022)	$249.99	$9,301.46
06/21/2022	Payment for claim 219325-0143	($102.74)	$9,198.72
06/30/2022	Payment for claim 219325-0146	($244.69)	$8,954.03
06/30/2022	Investment: Fund A	($1,043.10)	$7,910.93
06/30/2022	Investment: Fund B	($695.40)	$7,215.53
06/30/2022	Investment: Fund C	($1,043.13)	$6,172.40
06/30/2022	Investment: Fund D	($695.40)	$5,477.00
06/30/2022	Investment: Fund E	($695.40)	$4,781.60
06/30/2022	Investment: Fund F	($695.40)	$4,086.20
06/30/2022	Investment: Fund G	($695.40)	$3,390.80
06/30/2022	Investment: Fund H	($695.40)	$2,695.40
06/30/2022	Investment: Fund I	($695.40)	$2,000.00
06/30/2022	Interest for Jun-19 (Annual percentage yield earned for period is 1.25% on average collected balance of $8,864.03)	$9.18	$2,009.18
		Ending balance	$ 2,009.18

Investment portfolio

Fund	Category	Shares	Closing price	Closing value
Fund A	Small Cap Fund	73.14	$18.71	$1,368.45
Fund B	Small Cap Stock Index	82.71	$16.34	$1,351.48
Fund C	Blue Chip Value	223.25	$9.10	$2,031.58
Fund D	Emerging Markets	34.82	$41.06	$1,429.71
Fund E	International Market Masters	93.76	$15.12	$1,417.65
Fund F	Appreciation Fund	43.90	$31.39	$1,378.02
Fund G	Capital Appreciation	66.34	$20.72	$1,374.56
Fund H	Equity Income Fund	69.49	$19.52	$1,356.44
Fund I	Large Cap Index	108.47	$18.89	$2,049.00
			Ending balance	$13,756.89

Tracking deductibles

The EOB you receive from your health plan will show your progress toward meeting the plan limits for the year. Make sure you know how to interpret the deductible information in the EOB and always try to work from the most recent statement so you can make the right decisions about your care and how to pay for it.

If you do not have an HSA administrator that integrates with your insurance company and gives you a history of all of the claims paid by your HSA, it takes more effort to track your payments.

Always reconcile the paperwork you receive from your health plan with statements from your HSA. If you have had a problem with your health plan or HSA, you may have to follow up with both your health plan and HSA administrators to correct the error in both accounts.

In-network vs. out-of-network care

Most plans that include provider networks apply different out-of-pocket limits, deductibles, or both, to in-network and out-of-network care. In most health plans, this doesn't matter to you unless you or your family have a particularly costly year.

In an HSA-qualified HDHP, however, your deductible may be half or more of your out-of-pocket limit, so you may be more likely to hit the out-of-pocket limit than in other health plans.

This means you may want to keep track of your in-network and out-of-network spending and adjust your provider choices if you are close to meeting one limit but not the other.

Example: Selecting a network provider

Raj has a self-only plan with a $1,700 out-of-pocket limit for in-network care and a $2,600 limit for out-of-network care.

In-network care is insured at 100%; out-of-network care at 80%. His plan's deductible is $1,700.

Raj has spent $1,600 so far this year for in-network care and $250 for out-of-network care. He is considering foot surgery that will cost $2,000.

He can choose an in-network provider or one out of his network. If he chooses an in-network provider, he will pay $100, no matter what price the provider has negotiated with his plan. If he chooses an out-of-network provider, he will pay $400 ($2,000 x 20% non-network coinsurance).

Recordkeeping

Tracking HSA usage

In all health plans, your plan only pays for what it covers. Typically, the covered services are outlined in the plan documents you get from your insurer or the summary plan description (SPD) you get from your employer.

By using an HSA, in contrast, a wide range of expenses can be paid for, limited only by HSA legislation and what is generally accepted by the IRS for itemized medical deductions.

You need to understand what the allowable uses are and back up your distributions with appropriate documentation and receipts. If you do not, you may face a 20% penalty plus taxes for unauthorized distributions. If you spend the money on items other than eligible medical expenses, you will also be required to pay income taxes on those expenses.

Keeping accurate records

Any home financial software or spreadsheet program can be used to help you budget and keep track of medical expenses. However, if you need to substantiate or contest a claim, you will need copies of the original documents—either a paper copy or an electronic file. Some HSA administrators provide mobile apps to conveniently photograph and store these documents.

Your HSA can pay for certain expenses that are not covered by your HSA-qualified HDHP. For example, your HSA can be used for chiropractic services that might not be covered by your health plan's benefits.

Keep your HSA records as long as the account remains open, even if you have moved your account to a different provider or you are no longer eligible to contribute.

Organizing HSA and HDHP records

You may choose to save and file hard copies of your statements and receipts. If so, consider using a simple multi-pocket folder or a three-ring binder with separators. Remember that you will need original documents, electronic copies, or photocopies of receipts in the event of an IRS audit.

Alternatively, you may prefer to manage your insurance-related paperwork electronically by scanning your documents and storing them on your computer or in the cloud. Financial reports provided by your HSA administrator or by household budget programs, such as Quicken, can help you track your expenses.

After you have picked your organization system, set up the following sections:

- **Bills and proofs of payment from in-network providers**
  In addition to the bills you receive, include canceled checks or credit card receipts for any bills you did not pay directly from your HSA.

- **Bills and proofs of payment from out-of-network providers**
  Again, include canceled checks or credit card receipts for any bills you did not pay directly from your HSA and copies of all bills.

- **EOBs from network providers**
  Arrange in reverse chronological order (most recent on top), so you can easily track your progress toward meeting your health plan's limits that may apply to your network care.

- **EOBs from out-of-network providers**
  Arrange in reverse chronological order to easily track your progress toward meeting any separate HDHP limits that may apply to out-of-network care. You may not need separate files for in-network and out-of-network care if your HDHP does not apply separate limits.

- Bills and proofs of payment for healthcare not covered by your health plan
  Retain receipts for costs incurred that your health plan does not cover (and therefore do not count toward your deductible), because your HSA can be used for expenses not covered by your health plan. For example, the cost of braille reading materials for a blind person or the cost for transportation to and from providers or to see a specialist in another city are potentially covered by your HSA.

- Statements from HSA trustee or custodian
  For ease of reference, you may want to arrange this part of your file in reverse chronological order so you see the most current statement first.

Label your file with the current year and set up a new file every year. This will make it easier to track bills and reimbursements as time passes.

Storing records electronically

If you choose to store your records electronically, we suggest you have both on-site and off-site backups (in case of disaster, your computer and on-site backup can both be damaged.) If you plan to store your back up in the cloud using any number of commercial services, note that these storages may not be encrypted, meaning hackers or the government may be able to see the contents you store there. Some HSA administrators, like HealthEquity, support long-term access to your claims and HSA transactions for future reference and reimbursement needs.

Disputing charges

If you get a bill that does not make sense, call your provider's office, the customer service number provided for your health plan, or both. If you receive an incorrect statement, resolve the issue as soon as you can.

Everybody makes mistakes and a busy medical practice in particular will be dealing with a large number of plans that change requirements frequently, as well as patients whose plans have changed. Keep track and follow up.

Disagreeing with your health plan

All health plans can experience claims-processing errors from time to time. An in-network provider's invoice might be incorrectly processed as out-of-network, or the birth date for a participant could be incorrectly recorded, resulting in a denial of benefits.

Because your progress toward meeting the year's deductible can be affected, it is recommended that you immediately follow up on any errors.

Disagreeing with your HSA statement

You've probably had an unauthorized charge appear on a credit card at some point. You do not have to be a victim of identity theft for this to happen—a simple processing error can put a charge on your account that belongs to someone else.

If your HSA custodian issues you a debit or credit-type card, review charges on your HSA just as you do the charges on your credit card statements.

Understand your rights to have a disputed charge investigated, removed, or both. If your HSA issues checks, understand your rights to stop payment on a check and learn what to do if you lose your checkbook. The laws governing checkbooks and debit cards are not the same. Therefore, your rights to dispute a claim will vary depending on how the account was used.

Meeting IRS requirements

Because your HSA enjoys tax advantages, the IRS determines how you can spend your money. You can wait as long as you want after an expense has been incurred to submit it to your HSA. However, no matter how old the expense is, you must be prepared to fully document it to the IRS in the year you claim it or receive the distribution, if necessary.

Meeting HSA-qualified HDHP deadlines

Your employer may change from an HSA-qualified HDHP offered by one company to one offered by another or may eliminate your HSA-qualified HDHP entirely and move to another plan design.

If you change health plans, be sure any expenses you accrue are paid by the correct plan and coordinate your HSA with the new HSA-qualified HDHP. If your employer changes plans and you are no longer eligible to contribute to an HSA, you will not be able to contribute to your HSA as of the first day of the first month after the month your HSA-qualified HDHP coverage ends. For example, if your HSA-qualified HDHP coverage ends on June 15, you are no longer eligible to contribute to your HSA as of July 1. However, you can continue to use the funds in your HSA for qualified medical expenses.

Saving receipts and statements

You are responsible for documenting that your HSA distributions were made for qualified purposes. The HSA custodian or trustee, your insurer, and your employer are responsible for various aspects of your account reporting, but not this.

The IRS can generally audit most individual taxpayers for three years after the extended due date of the return.[2] This means if your income tax return for 2020 is due April 15, 2021, but you file for the automatic extension to August 15, the IRS can audit you until August 15, 2022.

In some situations, the audit period can be six years instead of three (for example, if you understate an item of income that is 25% or more than the total you have reported). Neither of these limitations applies if tax fraud or tax evasion is involved.[3]

It is suggested that you keep records documenting your HSA distributions for at least the period of time your income tax return is considered open or subject to audit, and preferably for as long as you maintain the account.

Even if your HSA provider gives you a debit card, credit card, or a checkbook, you may end up submitting claims yourself because you forgot to use the HSA, or because you may not have had enough money at the time of the expense to pay claims.

If you wait to organize your receipts, you may miss out on important benefits from your account and you may end up using post-tax dollars when HSA funds were available. However, for some this is a strategy used to preserve their account. Many HSA accountholders choose to pay for eligible expenses with after-tax dollars, shoe-boxing or filing eligible documentation until such time as they bundle those expenses for tax-free reimbursement.

Establish a clearly labeled file and keep track of what you have already submitted, what has been paid, and what is still outstanding. If your health plan offers online access to EOBs, get in the habit of using your plan website as a ready-made filing system.

Example: Lakeem saves his qualified medical expenses

Lakeem has been in an HSA-qualified HDHP for years and has a balance in his HSA

---

2   IRC §6501(a)
3   IRC §6501(e)(1)(A) (6 year rule), 6501(c) (fraud rule)

that exceeds $150,000. Lakeem is planning to retire but will wait to take Social Security until he is 70 to maximize his monthly benefit. Lakeem diligently pays any out-of-pocket expenses with after-tax funds and saves the documentation, keeping a running total of healthcare expenses he can be reimbursed for from his HSA. Just before Lakeem retires at age 69, he requests a distribution of $75,000 to reimburse expenses he previously paid with after-tax dollars. This amount is equal to Lakeem's take-home pay for the year, funding his first year of retirement and preserving Social Security benefits until they reach their maximum benefit level.

Paying taxes

Deductions

Your employer will report employer HSA contributions on your Form W-2. Your HSA trustee or custodian will report distributions to you and the IRS on Form 1099-SA and contributions on Form 5498-SA.

Eligibility for tax deductions

The employer, employee, or individual (if the HSA accountholder), depending on who makes the contribution, may claim deductions for HSA contributions. HSAs qualify as a deduction for federal and most state taxes.

Deducting contributions from others

Although parties other than the account holder or their employer can make contributions to the account holder's HSA, those third parties cannot deduct the contribution from their taxes.

However, the account holder who received the contribution can deduct the contribution from his or her gross income.

Example: Contributing to an adult child's HSA

Mindy and Maria's 25-year-old son Carlos attends college. Carlos is too old to qualify as a tax dependent, but young enough to be covered by his parents' HDHP

Mindy helps Carlos open his own HSA and makes a $1,000 contribution to the HSA.

Mindy and Maria cannot deduct the $1,000 on their own tax return, but Carlos can exclude it from his gross income.

Income tax deductions for the employee or individual purchaser

The tax-deductible contribution amount is calculated on a month-to-month basis, based on the total amount of the deduction and the number of months of participation.

The contribution is an above-the-line deduction for the purpose of calculating adjusted gross income, unless done through a cafeteria plan, where contributions are made on a pre-tax basis.

Example: HSA contribution as an above-the-line deduction

Hank, a single taxpayer, makes $36,000 a year and contributes $1,000 to his HSA.

On his tax return, he can only deduct medical expenses that exceed 7.5% of his adjusted gross income if he itemizes his deductions on Schedule A.

Hank has not had any medical expenses for the year. He decides that it is better to take an above-the-line deduction by subtracting the $1,000 HSA contribution when calculating his adjusted gross income.

Double-dipping is not allowed

You cannot count an HSA contribution twice by calculating it against your gross income and then deducting it as an itemized medical expense. In fact, no expense can be deducted twice or paid twice from different tax-exempt accounts or through different insurance plans.

However, as an eligible individual, you can deduct a contribution on your tax return even if another person makes it on your behalf.[4]

4   IRS Notice 2004-2 Q&A 18

Contributions

Employer-provided coverage

Contributions an employer makes to the employee's HSA are treated as employer-provided coverage for medical expenses under an accident or health plan and are excludable from the employee's gross income if made on behalf of an eligible individual.[5]

Employer contributions are not subject to income tax withholding from wages or to the Federal Insurance Contributions Act (FICA), the Federal Unemployment Tax Act (FUTA), or the Railroad Retirement Tax Act.

Employer contributions may be subject to certain state taxes.

Self-employed individuals and owners of S corporations

Self-employed individuals and 2-percent shareholder-employees of S corporations are not considered employees. As such, they cannot receive employer contributions. However, they can make their own contributions and claim the above-the-line deduction on their personal income tax return.

Contributions to the HSA made by a bona fide partner are treated as a distributive share of partnership income and they are considered guaranteed payments derived from the partnership's trade or business and are reported as such on IRS Schedule–K1 (Form 1065). The contributions are included in the partner's net earnings from which the partner is then able to deduct those contributions as an adjustment to gross income, just as any HSA owner is able to do within the confines of the law.

Contributions to the HSA of a greater than 2-percent shareholder-employee in consideration for services rendered are treated as a guaranteed payment, and are includable in the greater than 2-percent shareholder-employee's net earnings. The contributions can then be deducted as an adjustment to gross income.

---

5   IRS Notice 2004-2 Q&A 19

General tax forms

Wage and tax statement (W-2)

Employers must generally file a W-2 Form for any employee who was paid wages in a given year. Employees must enclose a copy of this form with federal, state, and local income tax returns. Your employer must report employer contributions (which include pre-tax cafeteria plan contributions to your HSA) in Box 12 on your W-2 Form. This should be coded W according to the instructions.

US individual income tax return (Form 1040)

If your HSA contributions exceed the legal limit ($3,600/$7,200 for individuals or families in 2021), the excess increases your adjusted gross income (AGI). Enter your post-tax HSA contributions on Form 1040 to calculate your AGI. Also include distributions made for anything other than qualified medical expenses.

Specific medical and Health Savings Account forms

The amounts reported on Forms 5498-SA and 1099-SA must agree with what you report on Form 1040.

Contributions to Medical Savings Accounts (Form 5498-SA)

Your HSA trustee or custodian will report HSA contributions to both you and the IRS on Form 5498-SA. This form also covers other Medical Savings Accounts: HSAs, Archer MSAs, and Medicare Advantage MSAs (MA MSAs).

Distributions from Medical Savings Accounts (Form 1099-SA)

Your HSA trustee or custodian will report HSA distributions to both you and the IRS on Form 1099-SA. For this reason, keep accurate records so you can prove the legality of your HSA distributions. Form 1099-SA also covers other Medical Savings Accounts: HSAs, Archer MSAs, and Medicare Advantage MSAs (MA MSAs).

HSAs (Form 8889)

You must file Form 8889 with Form 1040 or Form 1040NR if you (or your spouse, if married and filing a joint return) had any activity in your HSA during the year (contributions or distributions.) You must file the form even if the only contributions to your HSA came from your employer or your spouse's employer.

Complete a separate Form 8889 for each HSA if, during the tax year, you are the beneficiary of two or more HSAs, or you are a beneficiary of an HSA and you have your own HSA. Enter "statement" at the top of each Form 8889 and complete the form as instructed. Next, complete a controlling Form 8889 combining the amounts shown on each of the statement Forms 8889. Attach the statements to your tax return after the controlling Form 8889. If you and your spouse both have HSAs, you will need to complete separate forms for each; there is no joint Form 8889.[6]

Taxable contributions and distributions (Form 5329)

The calculations on Form 5329 will help you determine if you made contributions to or distributions from your HSA beyond the IRS-established limits. Also, if you experienced a significant life event, such as a divorce, this form can help you determine if your change in coverage caused additional tax liability.

If you have taxable HSA-related income, you will not only pay income taxes, but penalties as well: 6% for excess contributions and 20% for non-qualified distributions in 2021. If your calculations show that you owe tax or penalties on non-qualified distributions or excess contributions, you must file this form with your income tax return.

Summary

- You have several ways to pay for healthcare expenses:

  - Your in-network provider submits a claim to your health plan for goods or services rendered.

  - You file the claim yourself.

  - You use a debit card to spend from your HSA, or you request reimbursement from your HSA.

  - You submit expenses to your HSA-qualified FSA or HRA instead of your HSA for reimbursement. Spending from a use-it-or-lose-it account enhances the tax advantage of your HSA.

- Set up a well-organized filing system for invoices, point-of-sale receipts, explanation of benefits (EOB), and HSA statements. Either store physical documents or electronic copies.

- You can pay for a wider range of expenses with your HSA than your health plan covers. Familiarize yourself with the rules (which change from time to time) to maximize your benefit.

- In addition to ensuring the accuracy of your records, use your records to track your progress toward your deductible to make wise decisions about the timing of larger non-emergency expenditures.

- Good recordkeeping protects you from surprises—like the unexpected arrival of a delayed bill.

CHAPTER 10

Employer Benefits

Chapter overview

Employers who make HSAs available for their employees tend to see lower insurance rate increases. Because the overall cost of coverage is lower, the employer's share of the premiums is lower.

The number of HSAs and the total funds contributed to HSAs grows each year, suggesting that more employers offer HSA-qualified plans to save money and help them comply with the PPACA's health reform requirements. By using a thoughtful implementation strategy, employers can gain momentum and achieve significant savings.

While employers save money, they also take on some administrative responsibility—first to set up the plan, and then to maintain its tax-exempt status.

HSA benefits

Combatting rising costs

According to data published by the Centers for Medicare and Medicaid Services (CMS) in 2020, health spending has risen from $74.1 billion in 1970 to $3.8 trillion in 2019.[1] In 50 years, spending has increased 500-fold, well beyond cost-of-living increases.

Why the huge increase?

- New technologies and treatments increase life expectancy.

- More patients have chronic illnesses.

- Patients do not shop for lower-cost options (such as generic drugs).

- Patients over-utilize healthcare facilities (such as emergency rooms for minor illnesses).

- Administrative costs are passed on to consumers.

- State and federal governments require extended coverage.

Employers have control over only some of these variables. Specifically, they can influence healthcare usage patterns, help prevent chronic diseases through wellness programs, and perhaps lower the average cost of claims. Increased HSA adoption can potentially slow the trend of rising insurance rates by rewarding positive employee behavior.

Increasing awareness

Our healthcare system often separates the acts of receiving medical services and paying for them. A third party—the insurance company, employer, or plan administrator—usually processes and pays the bill, so consumers have little awareness of the actual price of medical services and products. Because the consumer only sees the amount of the copayment, not the full price for office visits, lab tests, etc., they may assume that the copayment covers the entire cost.

---

[1] https://www.cms.gov/Research-Statistics-Data-and-Systems/Statistics-Trends-and-Reports/NationalHealthExpendData/NHE-Fact-Sheet

As services become more expensive, consumers pay for the increased costs indirectly, through higher premiums. Again, the indirect connection between rising costs and rising premiums obscures the actual cost of goods and services. Only by understanding the actual price can consumers effectively comparison shop.

Increasing consumer choice

An HSA-qualified HDHP can encourage consumer choice by increasing incentives for consumers to compare costs and demand better value. Because HSA owners save on taxes and keep some of the savings achieved by careful consumerism, they have even more incentive to take an active role in controlling healthcare costs. This can theoretically lower the average cost of claims through better utilization of healthcare services, which would in turn lower premium costs.

Employers may use the savings achieved through HSA strategies to fund additional benefits for their employees, like wellness programs.

HSA implementation

As more and more employees choose an HDHP/HSA combination, employers see benefits—often to the point that they have more bargaining power to ask for lower rates from their insurance carriers. Additionally, they pay less payroll tax with increased employee contributions to HSAs.

Migrating gradually vs. full replacement

Some employers choose to offer their employees only one option for healthcare: an HSA-qualified HDHP. This full-replacement strategy significantly increases HSA ownership and the resulting savings.

Other employers, concerned about possible employee backlash or weakened ability to attract top employee talent, choose a gradual approach by offering multiple benefit plan choices that include one or more HSA-qualified HDHP options. These employers often set a goal to fully replace more traditional plans with HSA-qualified HDHPs within three to five years.

Employers have four primary motivators for adopting the more aggressive, full-replacement approach:

- Premium increases. Because of increasing premiums, they may need to reduce benefits to control costs. They can no longer afford traditional low-premium, low-out-of-pocket plans.

- Increase adoption rates. Cost projection tools make a case for rapid adoption:

  Increase HSA adoption → Lower premiums → Reduce cost trend → Contribute more to employees' HSAs → Increase HSA adoption…

- Increase ancillary benefits. When all employees have HSAs, more of them use low-cost services such as wellness programs, wellness incentives, telemedicine, and cost-transparency tools.

- Lower costs. Higher HSA adoption can reduce employer costs for healthcare.

Projecting savings

Let's look at a hypothetical company considering a consumer-driven healthcare strategy, with the intent of maximizing HSA ownership. The company is very committed to helping their employees prepare for healthcare costs in retirement. They believe this strategy will provide savings for the company and also for their employees. In order to project savings for budget purposes, the company must consider the medical cost trend, utilization, tax savings, and adoption rate.

Medical cost trend

The medical cost trend (the percentage of increase in medical costs, year over year) tends to be less for HSA-qualified HDHPs than for standard plans. Studies project premium savings of 1.5% to 3% when moving to an HSA-qualified HDHP.[2]

Utilization

Utilization and consumer behavior can also influence savings because members in an HSA-qualified HDHP tend to be more attentive consumers, seeking medical care less often and spending less when they do. This ultimately reduces overall healthcare spending.

---

2   Mercer's National Survey of Employer-Sponsored Health Plans 2020: Survey Report, page 10

Tax savings

HSA contributions reduce tax liabilities and can also contribute significantly to employers' savings.

- Employers save money on payroll taxes when they contribute to their employees' HSAs.

- Employees save on income and FICA taxes when they contribute to their own HSAs.

Adoption rate

Company savings also depends on how quickly employees adopt the HDHP/HSA option. Quicker adoption enhances cost stability and increases overall savings, both by reducing spend and by minimizing annual cost increases.

In order to increase the rate of HSA adoption at your organization, consider the following issues:

- If you offer more health coverage choices, adopting a more gradual implementation strategy, more employees will choose traditional plans.

- Education is key! Often, employees with higher healthcare expenses enroll in the richest possible plan, without realizing that all plans cap out-of-pocket limits, protecting them from high out-of-pocket expenses. Many times, employees pay higher premiums (and the company pays higher premium costs) for the same protection under a more expensive plan.

Employees really have two choices:

- Pay higher premiums and contributions now with less protection for unexpected out-of-pocket expenses.

- Pay lower premiums and contributions now and save the difference for future out-of-pocket expenses—all while enjoying tax benefits and accruing interest.

The faster companies achieve full adoption, the sooner the HSA strategy achieves the momentum necessary to build savings for the employer and healthy HSA balances for employees.

Reducing perceived risk

HealthEquity, the nation's oldest and largest non-bank custodian of HSA funds, has conducted research among its client base and concluded that three main factors influence an employee's decision on whether to enroll in an HSA-qualified HDHP:

- Insufficient funds. Consumers express concern that they will incur major healthcare expenses before their HSA balance can cover their deductibles.

- Age. Consumers believe that only younger, relatively healthy people should consider HSA-qualified HDHPs.

- Perceived relative financial value of an HSA-qualified HDHP. Consumers do not believe they can build and keep a large enough balance to realize significant financial benefit.

Overall, employees express concern about high out-of-pocket expenses. Balanced against the perceived safety of a traditional low-deductible health plan, it can be difficult to encourage adoption quickly enough to build traction and see significant savings.

Increasing HSA adoption

Previous chapters have discussed how HSA-qualified HDHPs benefit both employees and employers; they have also described some misconceptions and barriers to adoption.

The single most effective way to encourage adoption is a full-replacement approach that offers only one plan option: the HSA-qualified HDHP. Couple this strategy with robust communication and financial incentives to enhance trust with your employees and increase the benefit to both your organization and your employees.

This section describes best practices in increasing HSA adoption. The chart at the end of the section summarizes how various practices affect adoption rates.

Reduce the number of plan options

HealthEquity clients who offer three or more plan options report that their employees consistently remain with the same plans. HSA adoption among those groups remains at 5% or less. On the other hand, employers that choose the full-replacement plan option, offering only HSA-qualified HDHPs, report higher rates of adoption. As an added benefit, this strategy seems to increase communication amongst employees, commenting on their healthcare options and educating one another, creating better educated healthcare consumers.

Increase employee premium differentials

When the premium of the HSA-qualified HDHP option remains at least 40% less than other plan options, HSA adoption increases significantly.

Reduce deductible levels

Keeping the deductible as low as possible reduces the perception of risk associated with HDHPs. HealthEquity has observed that most clients who achieve high adoption (greater than 30%) set the deductible of the HDHPs to less than $2,000/$4,000.

Reduce out-of-pocket maximum

Employers should also offer the lowest possible out-of-pocket maximum. Employees perceive less risk when employers set the out-of-pocket maximum level for the HSA-qualified HDHP option equal to other plans offered. Reducing employee risk and increasing employer contributions improves adoption rates, even when a company offers two or more plans to employees during open enrollment.

Increase HSA employer contribution

Offering a meaningful employer contribution to employees' HSAs encourages employees to choose an HSA-qualified plan. Enhancing the wealth-building aspect of an HSA-qualified HDHP reduces the perception of risk.

Offer an HSA-qualified HDHP as default

Make it easy for employees to choose the HSA-qualified HDHP by creating enrollment tools that are easy to use. If open enrollment provides more than one option, make the HSA-qualified HDHP the default choice.

Consider multiple HSA-qualified HDHPs

Consider different deductibles and out-of-pocket limits. For example, maybe one HSA-qualified plan has deductibles of $3,000 self-only/$6,000 family and out-of-pocket limits of $4,000 self only/$8,000 family, while another has deductibles of $2,000 self-only/$4,000 family with out-of-pocket limits of $3,500 self-only/$7,000 family.

Involve executive management

HealthEquity has noted that all successful client groups actively involve company executives in their communication campaigns. Robust campaigns should begin early (several months before open enrollment) and include executives by providing messages from them about their own enrollment in HSA-qualified HDHPs. Executives are uniquely positioned to enhance trust and build enthusiasm for HSA programs.

Educate and communicate

A smooth transition to HSA-qualified health plans requires an organized effort to educate employees, increasing their awareness of and comfort with HSAs.

Those who do not understand how the tax savings and premium decreases compare financially to a higher deductible may consider an HSA-qualified HDHP a reduction in benefits. In order to communicate the true value, employers must help employees understand how the new plan works, help them with the financial decision involved in participating, and teach them how to contribute and how to make payments.

Additionally, employees need to know how much to contribute to an HSA, how to keep records, who to ask when they have questions, how to check HSA balances, how to use a network, and how to find good healthcare information. The HSA administrator and health plan may have tools to help employers educate their employees.

Employers who provide employees with information and tools to help them make better healthcare decisions, especially decisions on how to use the healthcare system effectively, will benefit their employees. HSA owners can increase the equity in HSA accounts and save on their taxes.

Employers and their HSA providers should conduct employee education and communication activities throughout the plan year—not just prior to open enrollment.

	Low Adoption	Medium Adoption	High Adoption
Number of healthcare plan options available	≥3	2	1 (only HDHP)
Employee premium differential vs. traditional plan	≤15%	16%–39%	≥40%
Deductible level	>$2K/$4K single/family	Up to $2K /$4K	Federally mandated minimum
Out-of-pocket max, compared to traditional plans	>51% higher	0–50% higher	Equal to
HSA employer contribution (as percentage of deductible)	≤25%	26%–59%	≥60%
Active vs. passive enrollment	Passive, non-HDHP default	N/A	Active, HSA-qualified HDHP default
Executive involvement	None	Endorse HDHPs	Executives choose HDHPs
Communication strategy	Limited or none	Moderate 0–2 months	Active ≥6 months

HSA rules and regulations

In order for employees to retain tax benefits and for employers to avoid penalties, companies must adhere to several IRS guidelines regarding HSAs. Specifically, employer contributions to employees' HSAs must pass a nondiscrimination test. In some instances, contributions must also adhere to a comparability test.

Nondiscrimination

Nondiscrimination rules forbid companies from providing greater benefits to highly compensated employees (HCEs) and key employees (those with major ownership or decision-making authority) than they do to lower-paid employees. These nondiscrimination rules apply to most benefits offered by employers, such as 401(k)s and FSAs.[3]

---

3   Treas. Reg. §54.4980G-5 Q&A 1, IRC §125(b), (c) and (g)

Nondiscrimination testing includes three key concepts:

- Eligibility—the plan must cover a high enough percentage of non-HCEs

- Contributions—HCEs cannot receive disproportionately more contributions than non-HCEs

- Benefits—HCEs cannot have access to more plan features than non-HCEs

Comparability

The best way for an employer to make contributions to employee-owned HSAs is through a Section 125 cafeteria plan (which is exempt from the comparability testing described here). However, if employers choose to make direct contributions to employees' HSA, the contributions must adhere to comparability rules.

Comparability rules require that employers contribute the same dollar amount (or the same percentage of the annual deductible amount) to all HSA owners who have the same employment status (such as full-or part-time) and the same category of coverage (such as self-only or family.)[4] Failure to follow comparability requirements could result in a 35% excise tax on employer contributions.

This means that all individuals within each of the four categories listed below must receive comparable contributions from their employer:

- Part-time employee with self-only coverage

- Part-time employee with family coverage

- Full-time employee with self-only coverage

- Full-time employee with family coverage

Note that the actual categories may differ (for example, categories might include self-plus-one coverage), but the principle of providing comparable contributions within each category always applies.

---

4   IRC §4980G, Treas. Reg. §54.4980G-5 Q&A 1 and 2

One company might pass the comparability test if each eligible full-time self-only employee receives $500 toward their HSA and each full-time family-covered employee receives $750. Another company makes comparable contributions if all part-time employees receive funds equal to 75% of their deductible.

Remember that if a married couple works for the same employer, their HSAs and the contributions made to their accounts must remain completely separate. To do otherwise risks violating comparability rules because if one spouse receives the contribution for themselves as well as for their spouse, they would receive twice the contribution of some other employees.[5]

Non-HCE exception

One exception to the comparability rule described above exists: employers may contribute more to the HSAs of non-highly compensated employees (non-HCEs).[6] The IRS uses the same definition for HCEs here as they do for other retirement accounts: $130,000 for tax years 2020 and 2021.[7]

Exception for cafeteria plan HSAs

Because cafeteria plan HSAs do not need to adhere to comparability rules, employers may match employee contributions or require an employee to contribute to their HSA before also contributing.

5   Treas. Reg. §54.4980G-3 Q&A 8
6   IRC §4980G(e), Treas. Reg. §54-4980G-4, Treas. Reg. §54.4980G-6
7   IRC §4980G(e), Treas. Reg. §54.4980G-6

The table below summarizes these guidelines.

	HSA as part of a cafeteria plan	HSA outside of a cafeteria plan
Employee contributions	Pre-tax contributions (saves money on payroll taxes) May be required to contribute in order to receiver employer funds	Post-tax contributions are deducted (above-the-line) from income on federal tax return May receive employer funds without contributing
Employer contributions	Pre-tax contributions through employer-sponsored plan	Allowed as tax-free employer-provided benefits
Rules	Nondiscrimination rule[8] applies	Both nondiscrimination and comparability rules[9] apply
Matching contributions	Permitted	Not permitted

If employer contributions fail the comparability test, they are subject to a 35% excise tax on employer contributions.[10]

Notice to employees

The notice requirement only applies to cafeteria-plan HSAs.

Through a cafeteria plan, employers may require employees to contribute to their HSA before the employer makes a contribution.[11] For example, through a cafeteria plan, an employer may offer to contribute $500 to employees' accounts on the condition that they also make a contribution to the account.

Under the notice requirement, employers must notify employees that each eligible employee who establishes an HSA by the last day of February and notifies their employer will receive a comparable contribution to the HSA for the prior year.

Employers will meet the notice requirement if, by January 15 (the month before the end-of-February deadline), they provide written notice to all affected employees.[12]

---

8 Eligibility, contributions and benefits must not favor highly compensated individuals
9 Similar employees receive equivalent employer contributions
10 IRC §4980G, Treas. Reg. §54.4980G-1, Q&A 4
11 Treas. Reg. §54.4980G-4 Q&A-8; Treas. Reg. §54.4980G-5
12 Treas. Reg. §54.4980G-4 Q&A 14

Employers will meet the contribution requirement (described in the previous section) for these employees if, by April 15 or an IRS-specified deadline, they contribute comparable amounts plus reasonable interest to the employees' HSAs for the prior year.[13]

Required reporting

HSA owners must receive periodic statements that include HSA balances, interest earned, investment returns, fees and administrative expenses (for example, maintenance fees and check replacement), and expenses paid out of the HSA.

Oversight: ERISA, DOL, IRS

Two government agencies oversee most of the federal regulation of private employer benefit plans: the US Department of Labor and the IRS.

The Employee Retirement Income Security Act (ERISA), enforced by both the IRS and the DOL, established legal guidelines for the administration and investment practices of private employer benefit plans.

ERISA generally preempts state laws that apply to private-sector employee benefit plans. In that case, state laws do not apply to employee benefit plans, even if state law sets higher standards of benefits than what the plan offers.[14]

The Department of Labor (DOL) enforces participants' benefit rights under ERISA, and the IRS ensures that employers meet the tax code that applies to sponsoring benefit plans and deducting associated costs.

The DOL protects healthcare benefits, but they do not consider HSAs an employee benefit plan (for which ERISA regulations apply). Instead, as a personal healthcare savings vehicle, state laws (rather than group insurance regulations) apply to HSAs.[15]

This safe harbor exemption from ERISA for HSAs exists even if the employer makes contributions to the HSA, unless the HSA fails to meet any of the following requirements:

---

13   Treas. Reg. §54.4980G-4 Q&A 2(f)
14   ERISA §514, with the exception of Hawaii's healthcare laws enacted before 1974
15   DOL Field Assistance Bulletin 2004-1, 2006-2

- The employer must allow eligible employees to move their funds to another HSA, while adhering to Internal Revenue Code (IRC) restrictions.

- The employer may not impose conditions on utilization of HSA funds beyond the IRC's restrictions.

- The employer cannot make or influence investment decisions with respect to funds contributed to the HSA.

- The employer cannot represent the HSA as an employee welfare benefit plan established or maintained by the employer.

- The employer may not receive any payment or compensation in connection with the HSA.

Failure to meet one of these requirements can trigger ERISA oversight. Otherwise, an HSA is subject to state law.

Implications

Because HSAs are generally not subject to ERISA rules, they lack protection in the event of personal bankruptcy. Most other retirement savings plans are shielded from creditors. For example, when an account holder accumulates funds in an employer-sponsored pension plan or 401(k), creditors may not seize the funds if the account holder declares personal bankruptcy.

Also, states' unclaimed properties law (also known as escheat laws) apply to non-ERISA HSAs. If your account lies dormant for a period of time, the trustee or custodian must forward the amount to the State's treasury, which will hold it until the account owner claims it back. To prevent this, you need to keep your account active by checking the balance periodically. Check with your custodian for state-specific regulations.

Governmental employer plans

The Office of Personnel Management (OPM), not ERISA, enforces federal employee benefit laws for federal, state, and local government employers. For this reason, there may be less consistency regarding reporting, comparability, eligibility, fiduciary obligations, and recordkeeping.

Summary

- Employers receive tax benefits when their employees have HDHPs and HSAs and tend to pay less in overall healthcare costs.

- Increased adoption provides more savings opportunities for employees and employers. The most efficient strategy is to offer only HSA-qualified HDHPs. Enhance the effectiveness of the strategy by reducing deductible levels and out-of-pocket maximums, increasing communication, and obtaining executive management buy-in.

- HSAs (and other retirement savings plans) must pass nondiscrimination testing: highly compensated employees and key employees may not benefit disproportionately.

- In addition to the non-discrimination rule, non-cafeteria plan HSAs must also comply with the comparability rule, which requires equivalent employer contributions for all similar employees. Cafeteria-plan HSAs are exempt from the comparability rule, which allows them to provide employer matching contributions or to require that employees contribute to an HSA before their employer does.

- Three agencies oversee employee health benefits: The Employee Retirement Income Security Act (ERISA) establishes individuals' benefit rights; the DOL enforces the rights; and the IRS ensures that employers meet the relevant tax code.

- Because the DOL does not consider HSAs an employee benefit plan (but rather a personal healthcare savings vehicle), state law applies to HSAs.

APPENDIX A

Glossary of health insurance and tax-related terms

Above-the-line deduction

A deduction that can be taken from gross income before arriving at adjusted gross income (AGI). Examples include IRA contributions, HSA contributions, half of the self-employment tax, the self-employed health insurance deduction, and alimony. The term is derived from a solid bold line on Form 1040 and 1040A above the line for adjusted gross income. A taxpayer can take deductions above the line and still choose whether to claim the standard deduction or itemize deductions.

Annual limit

A dollar limit on the claims an insurer will pay over the course of a plan year. The Patient Protection and Affordable Care Act (PPACA) prohibits annual limits for essential benefits for plan years beginning after September 23, 2010.

Authorization

A health insurance plan's permission to proceed with a medical or surgical procedure.

Balance billing

A bill that the participant receives for the portion of an out-of-network provider's bill that the insurance plan doesn't cover. When a participant receives services from a healthcare provider that doesn't participate in the insurer's network, the healthcare provider isn't obligated to accept the insurer's payment as payment in full, and they can bill the participant for the unpaid amount.

Cafeteria plan

An employee benefit plan that allows employees to choose benefits from among a number of different options, including pensions, FSAs, health insurance, other insurance, and paid time off.

Calendar year

January 1 to December 31 of the same year. The calendar year may be different than the plan year; the latter may be any 12-month period established by an employer or insurer for managing the plan and accounting for benefit payments.

Certificate of coverage

Written evidence of prior health coverage—required under HIPAA—and provided by the insurer once coverage ends. An enrollee may need to provide this certificate to be exempt from limitations on coverage for pre-existing conditions. In most situations, the PPACA has eliminated the need for this certificate by prohibiting denial of coverage for pre-existing conditions.

Chronic condition

A condition that lasts indefinitely, or recurs frequently, and can be treated but not cured.

COBRA

Acronym for the Consolidated Omnibus Budget Reconciliation Act of 1985 that provides for the temporary continuation of group health plan coverage after a qualifying event to certain employees, retirees, and family members who are qualified beneficiaries. An HSA can be used to pay for COBRA premiums.

Coinsurance

The percentage of an insurance claim for which the patient is responsible to pay.

Comparable contributions

Employer contributions are considered comparable if the employer makes similar contributions on behalf of all eligible employees with similar coverage during the same period. Contributions are considered comparable if either the same dollar amount or the same percentage of the deductible under the HDHP.

Conversion coverage

Coverage under an individual insurance policy when group health plan benefits are lost. Employers that offer an individual conversion option to active employees must make that option available to COBRA-qualified beneficiaries as well.

Contribution (for HSA)

Deposit to the Health Savings Account (HSA).

Copayment

Fixed-dollar payments the patient makes for a doctor visit or prescription. For example, many HMOs and PPOs impose a copayment (sometimes referred to as a copay) for an in-network doctor's visit.

Covered services

The medically necessary treatments a plan pays for, at least in part.

Custodian

An entity responsible for the maintenance or administration of an account (such as an HSA or IRA) that has no investment or management responsibilities.

Deductible

The amount of covered expenses that an individual pays for out of pocket before payments are made by the health plan.

Dependent

For a health plan

A dependent that a health insurance company covers under an individual's health plan, not the same as a tax dependent.

In most cases, the health insurance company and state law decide who is a qualified dependent under the health plan. One exception is the federal mandate under the PPACA that adult children up to age 26 be covered by a parent's family plan if the child doesn't have access to health coverage from his or her own employer. This coverage is not taxable to the parent. However, the child can only receive distributions from the parent's HSA if the child also qualifies as a tax dependent on the parent's return. If the adult child is covered under a parent's family HDHP but doesn't qualify as a tax dependent, the child can open his or her own HSA.

For tax purposes

A person who can be claimed as a dependent on your federal tax return. This isn't the same as a dependent on your health plan. You can receive distributions from your HSA for qualified medical expenses paid only for your spouse and people you can claim as dependents on your tax return, whether or not they are covered by your family HDHP.

Distribution (for HSA)

Withdrawal from a Health Savings Account (HSA).

Eligible individual (for HSA)

An individual who meets all the IRS criteria for contributing to his or her own HSA.

Emergency

The sudden onset of a condition or an accidental injury requiring immediate medical or surgical care to avoid permanent disability or death.

Employee Assistance Plan/Program (EAP)

An employee benefit that covers all or part of the cost for employees to receive counseling, referrals, and advice in dealing with stressful life issues.

ERISA (Employee Retirement Income Security Act)

A federal law that governs private-sector employee benefits plans.

Excess contribution (for HSA)

An HSA contribution that's higher than allowed by the IRS.

Exchange

A government-regulated marketplace of insurance plans with different tiers, or levels of coverage, offered to individuals without healthcare or to small companies; also referred to as a health exchange.

The PPACA created new American Health Benefit Exchanges in each state to assist individuals and small businesses with comparing and purchasing qualified health insurance coverage.

Exclusions

Medical services or conditions for which a particular healthcare plan or policy won't pay.

First-dollar coverage

Benefits that pay the entire covered or eligible amount without requiring a deductible.

Flexible Spending Account (FSA)

An arrangement that allows employees to set aside pre-tax earnings to pay for expenses not covered by their insurance or benefit plans. May be free-standing or part of a cafeteria plan. All unspent funds are forfeited back to the employer at the end of the year unless the employer allows a rollover.

Formulary

The list of drugs covered fully or in part by a health plan.

Full contribution rule

Also called the last-month rule. See last-month rule and testing period.

Gatekeeper

The doctor, usually a primary care doctor, pediatrician or internist, responsible for overseeing and coordinating all aspects of a patient's care. In an HMO, the gatekeeper must preauthorize all referrals, except emergencies.

Grace period (for FSA)

The period when the account holder can continue to incur expenses and submit reimbursements after the end of the plan year. After the end of the grace period, any unused balances for the previous plan year are forfeited back to the employer.

Grandfathered plan

A health plan that an individual was enrolled in prior to the passage of the PPACA on March 23, 2010.

Grandfathered plans are exempt from many of the immediate changes required by the PPACA. New employees may be added to group plans that are grandfathered, and new family members may be added to all grandfathered plans.

Healthcare reform law

See Patient Protection and Affordable Care Act (PPACA).

Health Insurance Portability and Accountability Act (HIPAA)

A federal law that limits the exclusion of pre-existing conditions, permits special enrollment when certain life or work events occur, prohibits discrimination against employees and dependents based on health status, and guarantees availability and renewability of health coverage to certain employees and individuals. It also establishes strict standards for using and sharing private health information (PHI).

Health Reimbursement Arrangement (HRA)

An employer-owned and funded account from which the employee is reimbursed for qualified medical expenses, such as copayments, deductibles, vision care, prescriptions, long-term care, medical insurance, and most dental expenses. Reimbursements aren't taxed to the employee and are deductible by the employer.

High-deductible health plan (HDHP)

A type of health insurance plan that, compared to traditional health insurance plans, requires higher initial out-of- pocket spending, although premiums may be lower.

HIPAA

See Health Insurance Portability and Accountability Act (HIPAA).

HMO (health maintenance organization)

A corporate entity (for-profit or not-for-profit) that provides or arranges for coverage of certain health services for a fixed, prepaid premium.

Home healthcare

Skilled nursing and related care supplied to a patient at home.

Hospice care

Care given to terminally ill patients, generally those with six months or less to live and that emphasizes meeting emotional needs and coping with pain. Care may be given in the patient's home or at a facility.

Hospital outpatient department

A facility or area where a range of non- urgent medical care is provided under the supervision of a physician.

Indemnity plan

A plan that pays health insurance benefits in the form of cash payments rather than services.

Individual coverage requirements and penalties

Requirement for most individuals to obtain acceptable health insurance coverage or pay a penalty. There will be no penalty if affordable coverage is not available to an individual.

Individual Retirement Account (IRA)

An account that allows individuals to save for retirement on a tax-deferred basis. The amount that is tax deductible varies according to an individual's pension coverage, income tax filing status, and adjusted gross income.

In-network provider

A healthcare provider (such as a hospital or doctor) contracted to be part of the network for a managed care organization (such as an HMO or PPO). The provider agrees to the managed care organization's rules and fee schedules in order to be part of the network and agrees not to balance-bill patients for amounts beyond the agreed upon fee.

Last-month rule

IRS rule that allows a participant who enrolls in a qualifying HDHP mid-year to contribute the entire yearly maximum contribution for his or her age and coverage level if the participant opens an HSA-qualified HDHP by the first day of the last month of the tax year (December 1 for most taxpayers). Also referred to as the full contribution rule.

The participant must remain eligible for the entire testing period to avoid incurring taxes and penalties.

See testing period.

Life event

A change in a participant's personal situation that results in the gain or loss of eligibility for an HSA, a health plan, or a spouse's or dependent's employer's plan.

Participants who experience a qualified life event may be eligible to make changes to their benefit coverage. Life events include, but are not limited to:

- Marriage or beginning a domestic partnership

- Divorce or termination of a domestic partnership

- Birth or adoption of a child

- Death of a spouse, domestic partner, or child

- Spouse loses coverage

- Child loses eligibility

- Change in employment status

- Loss of qualified HDHP coverage

Lifetime limit

The limit many health plans place on the claims that the insurer will pay over the course of an individual's life. The PPACA prohibited lifetime limits on benefits beginning September 23, 2010.

Limited benefits plan

A type of health plan that provides coverage for only certain specified healthcare services or treatments or provides coverage for healthcare services or treatments for a certain amount during a specified period.

Managed care plan

A health plan that limits costs by limiting the reimbursement levels paid to providers and by monitoring healthcare utilization by participants or both.

Mandated benefit

A requirement in state or federal law that all health insurance policies provide coverage for a specific healthcare service.

Matching contributions

Employer contributions paid to the employee's account (HSA, FSA) only if the employee also contributes a minimum specified amount.

Medicare

A federal government health insurance program for people 65 and older, the disabled, and people with end-stage renal disease who require dialysis or a transplant. Part of the Social Security system.

- **Medicare Part A**. Pays for inpatient hospital stays, care in a skilled nursing facility, hospice care, and some home healthcare.

- **Medicare Part B**. Helps pay for doctors' services, outpatient hospital care, durable medical equipment, and some medical services not covered by Part A.

- **Medicare Part C** (Medicare Advantage Plans). A combination of Part A and Part B. The main difference in Part C is that it's provided through private insurance companies approved by Medicare.

- **Medicare Part D**. A stand-alone prescription drug coverage insurance.

Medicare Part D "donut hole"

The gap between the maximum spending amount Medicare Part D will cover and the minimum spending amount to qualify for catastrophic prescription drug coverage. The beneficiary is responsible for 100% of all costs between these two amounts.

Medicare supplement (Medigap) insurance

Private insurance that supplements Medicare and Medicare Advantage Plans. It reimburses out-of-pocket costs not covered by Medicare and that are the beneficiary's share of healthcare costs.

A participant can't have an HSA if he or she also has Medigap insurance.

Medical loss ratio

The percentage of health insurance premiums spent by the insurance company on actual healthcare services rather than administrative costs. The PPACA requires that large group plans spend 85% of premiums on clinical services and other activities for the quality of care for enrollees. Small group and individual market plans must devote 80% of premiums to these purposes.

Medically necessary treatments

Treatments appropriate for the diagnosis, care, or treatment of a certain injury or condition. Check the plan's definition; whether or not a given service is covered may depend on where and by whom it is delivered.

Mistaken distribution (for HSA)

Mistaken withdrawal from a Health Savings Account (HSA), such as a non-qualified medical expense or an over-payment to a healthcare provider. A participant can avoid paying income tax and a 20% penalty on the amount by returning the money to the HSA administrator for re-deposit into the HSA.

Multistate plan

A plan, created by the PPACA and overseen by the U.S. Office of Personnel Management (OPM), that has been available in every state through healthcare exchanges since 2014.

Network plan

A plan that generally provides more favorable benefits for services provided by its network of providers than for services provided outside the network.

Open enrollment

A period of time during which employees may change health plans without incurring costs or penalties.

Out-of-network provider

A healthcare provider (such as a hospital or doctor) that is not contracted to be part of a managed care organization's network (such as an HMO or PPO).

Depending on the managed care organization's rules, an individual may not be covered at all or may be required to pay a higher portion of the total costs when he or she seeks care from an out-of-network provider. A health plan may disallow applying out-of-network provider costs to the deductible.

Out-of-pocket limit

A maximum limit on the out-of-pocket expenses a participant pays during the plan year. Amounts a participant pays for deductibles, co- payments, or coinsurance are included in out-of-pocket expenses and kept as a running total. Insurance premiums aren't counted toward out-of-pocket limits.

Once a participant reaches the plan's limit for the year, remaining eligible expenses are covered at 100% regardless of the plan's copayment or coinsurance arrangements. Some plans refer to this limit as the stop-loss limit or out-of-pocket maximum.

Patient Protection and Affordable Care Act (PPACA)

Legislation (Public Law 111-148) signed by President Obama on March 23, 2010. Commonly referred to as the healthcare reform law.

Permitted coverage

Coverage an individual may maintain, in addition to an HDHP, without losing eligibility for an HSA, even though the coverage may provide first-dollar coverage for certain medical expenses.

PHI

Protected health information that is strictly protected by HIPAA.

Plan administrator

The person or firm designated by a health plan or employer to handle day-to-day details of recordkeeping, claims handling, and report filing.

Plan participant or beneficiary

An employee or dependent of that employee who is participating in, receiving benefits from, or eligible to receive benefits from an employee benefit plan.

Plan year

The calendar year (January 1 to December 31) or another 12-month period the employer or insurer chooses for managing a health plan and keeping track of deductibles and other limits.

Point of service (POS)

A managed care plan that allows patients to see doctors not included in the plan, but for an increased fee; usually found as part of an HMO.

Portable account

An account that can be carried from job to job and from group plans to individual coverage.

Pre-existing condition exclusion

A period of time when an individual receives no benefits under a health benefit plan for an illness or medical condition for which the individual received medical advice, diagnosis, care, or treatment within a specified period of time prior to the date of enrollment in the health benefit plan.

The PPACA prohibits pre-existing condition exclusions for all plans beginning January 2014.

Preferred provider organization (PPO)

An arrangement between doctors and other medical service providers and an insurer to offer services at a discounted rate in exchange for the insurer sending patients to their doctors or facilities. Usually includes some utilization review.

Premium

The periodic payment required to keep an insurance policy in force.

Preventive benefits

Covered services intended to prevent or identify a medical condition while it is more easily treatable. The PPACA requires insurers to provide coverage for preventive benefits without charging deductibles, copayments, or coinsurance.

Primary payer

The healthcare plan that pays its share of covered expenses first when a consumer has access to two different health plans, while the secondary payer pays some or all of the amount left over—even if that amount is less than the secondary plan otherwise pays. This applies to Medicare when the participant is still covered under an employer plan.

Prohibited transaction

The sale, exchange, or lease of property; borrowing or lending money; furnishing goods, services, or facilities; transferring to, used by, or for the benefit of the HSA account beneficiary of any assets contained in the account. Pledging account assets—as security for a loan, for example—constitutes a prohibited transaction.

Provider

Whoever provides healthcare under a health plan, including doctors, therapists, nurse-practitioners, and anyone else who provides medical services.

Provider discount

The reduced rate a doctor, hospital, or other healthcare professional or facility agrees to accept when they enroll in a health plan's network.

Prudent layperson standard

Under this standard, emergency care is covered in a healthcare plan if the decision to go to the ER was one that an average person with average medical knowledge would make at the time.

Qualified health plan

A health insurance policy sold through an exchange. The PPACA requires exchanges to certify that qualified health plans meet minimum standards outlined in the law.

Qualified medical expense

An expense paid by the account beneficiary or owner, his or her spouse, or his or her dependents, for medical care as defined in §213(d) of the Internal Revenue Code; generally, the same expense that individual taxpayers can deduct on federal income tax returns.

Certain types of health insurance premiums are considered a qualified medical expense for purposes of HSAs.

Referral

A recommendation of a medical professional. In HMOs and other managed care plans, a referral is usually necessary to see any practitioner or specialist other than a gatekeeper physician for the service to be covered.

Release

Permission for specified medical information to be released to a specific person or entity.

Repricing

The adjustment of healthcare providers' "sticker price" to reflect discounts the providers may have negotiated with a health plan.

Rescission

The process of voiding a health plan from its inception usually based on the grounds of material misrepresentation or omission on the application for insurance coverage that would have resulted in a different decision by the health insurer with respect to issuing coverage. The PPACA prohibits rescissions except in cases of fraud or intentional misrepresentation of a relevant fact.

Rollover contribution

Distribution of an account balance from one financial institution and re-depositing it in another, or from one type of account (MSA) to another (HSA).

Safe harbor

When an activity is deemed to meet certain authorized criteria, it will be safe and considered in compliance with law or regulation.

Screening services

Medical tests designed to detect treatable diseases or conditions.

Section 401(k) plan

A defined contribution retirement plan that allows participants to have a portion of their compensation (otherwise payable in cash) contributed pre-tax to a retirement account on their behalf. The plan is named after the section of the Internal Revenue Code that establishes the rules for the plan.

Self-insured plan

A plan under which the employer pays for medical claims as they arise rather than contracting for coverage from an insurer.

Stop-loss limit

See out-of-pocket limit.

Testing period

The length of time an individual must remain in a qualified HDHP to avoid taxes and penalties if he or she makes the maximum yearly contribution to an HSA under the last-month rule.

If the individual enrolled in a qualifying HDHP mid-year but contributed the full yearly maximum contribution to the HSA under the last-month rule, he or she must remain an eligible individual during the testing period. For the last-month rule, the testing period begins with the last month of the tax year and ends on the last day of the twelfth month following that month. For example, December 1, 2018, through December 31, 2019. See last-month rule.

Transition rule

A gradual adaptation to a law in order to ease the impact of a change on affected taxpayers.

Trend

Medical cost inflation; for example, the yearly increase in the cost of premiums.

Trust

Legal instrument allowing one party (the trustee) to control property for the benefit of another.

Trustee

An entity or individual that directs the investment of the funds in a trust account and has management responsibilities.

Umbrella deductible

A stated maximum amount of expenses a family could incur before receiving benefits.

Usual, customary, and reasonable charge (UCR)

The cost associated with a healthcare service that's consistent with the going rate for identical or similar services within a particular geographic area.

Reimbursement for out-of-network providers is often set at a percentage of the usual, customary, and reasonable charge, which may differ from what the provider actually charges for a service.

Waiting period

A period of time that an individual must wait, either after becoming employed or submitting an application for a health insurance plan, before coverage becomes effective and claims may be paid.

Premiums aren't collected during this period and HSA contributions can't begin until the first day of the month after the waiting period ends and HDHP coverage begins.

APPENDIX B

IRS forms[1]

US individual income tax return

- Form 1099-SA: www.irs.gov/pub/irs-pdf/ f1099sa.pdf

- Form W-2 (includes a section for HSA reporting): www.irs.gov/pub/irs-pdf/fw2.pdf

- Form 1040/1040EZ: www.irs.gov/pub/irs-pdf/f1040.pdf

Distributions from an HSA, Archer MSA, or Medicare Advantage MSA

- Form 5329: www.irs.gov/pub/irs-pdf/f5329.pdf

Additional taxes on qualified plans (including IRAs) and other tax-favored accounts

- Form 5498-SA: www.irs.gov/pub/irs-pdf/f5498sa.pdf

HSA, Archer MSA, or Medicare Advantage MSA information

- Form 5305b: www.irs.gov/pub/irs-pdf/f5305b.pdf

Health savings trust account

- Form 5305c: www.irs.gov/pub/irs-pdf/f5305c.pdf

---

1   See www.irs.gov for full details. For recent updates, see www.hsaguidebook.com

APPENDIX C
Qualified medical expenses

The IRS provides yearly updates on the medical and dental expenses that are and are not tax-deductible. See www.irs.gov for the most current version of Publication 502: Eligible Medical and Dental Expenses.

The following is a list of items that can be included in calculating the medical expense deduction. Items are listed in alphabetical order and, if listed, the amount paid by a participant can be included as a medical expense.

IRS Publication 502 discusses items that are eligible for tax deductions. Not all the items on this list may be reimbursed by an FSA, HRA, or HSA. Each of those accounts will reimburse for most of the items on this list, but not all of them. The lists for the various types of accounts are not identical.

Abortion

Acupuncture

Alcoholism

Inpatient treatment at a therapeutic center for alcohol addiction, including meals and lodging provided by the center during treatment; amounts paid for transportation to and from Alcoholics Anonymous meetings if attendance is pursuant to medical advice that membership in Alcoholics Anonymous is necessary for the treatment of patient's alcoholism.

Ambulance services

Artificial limb

Artificial teeth

Bandages

Birth control pills

Braille books and magazines

For use by a visually impaired person that is more than the cost of regular printed editions.

Breast reconstruction surgery

Following a mastectomy for cancer or other breast disease.

Capital expenses

Special equipment installed in a home and other home improvements if the main purpose is medical care for yourself, your spouse, or your dependent. The cost of permanent improvements that increase the value of a property may be partly included as a medical expense. The cost of the improvement is reduced by the increase in the value of the property. The difference is a medical expense. If the value of the property is not increased by the improvement, the entire cost is included as a medical expense.

Certain improvements made to accommodate a home for a disabled person don't usually increase the value of the home, and the cost can be included in full as medical expenses. These improvements include, but aren't limited to, the following:

- Constructing entrance or exit ramps

- Widening doorways at entrances or exits

- Widening or otherwise modifying hallways and interior doorways

- Installing railings, support bars, or other modifications to bathrooms

- Lowering or modifying kitchen cabinets and equipment

- Moving or modifying electrical outlets and fixtures

- Installing porch lifts and other forms of lifts (elevators generally add value to the house)

- Modifying fire alarms, smoke detectors, and other warning systems

- Modifying stairways

- Adding handrails or grab bars anywhere (whether or not in bathrooms)

- Modifying hardware on doors

- Modifying areas in front of entrance and exit doorways

- Grading the ground to provide access to the residence

Only reasonable costs to accommodate a home for a disabled person are considered medical care. Additional costs for general repair or aesthetic reasons aren't medical expenses.

Example: Making capital improvements on a home

Stephen and Andrea are taking care of an elderly parent who has had a stroke.

All the bedrooms and bathrooms in their home are on the second floor. They install an elevator and modify one bathroom to accommodate a wheelchair.

The elevator costs $8,000. An appraisal shows that the elevator increases the value of their home by $4,400.

They subtract the increased value of their home ($4,400) from the cost of the improvement ($8,000). The difference ($3,600) is the amount they can claim as a medical expense.

Construction to widen the doorway of a bathroom and replace the bathtub with a wheelchair-accessible shower costs $5,800. Because the bathroom remodel doesn't increase the value of their home, the owners can claim the entire $5,800 as a medical expense.

Operation and upkeep

Amounts paid for the operation and upkeep of a capital asset, as long as the main reason is for medical care; applies even if none or only part of the original cost of the capital asset qualifies as a medical care expense.

Example: Improvements that increase the value of a home

If, in the previous example, the elevator increased the value of the home by $8,000, the owners wouldn't be able to claim any portion of the cost of the elevator as a qualified medical expense.

However, the cost of electricity to operate the elevator and any costs to maintain it are medical expenses as long as the medical reason for the elevator exists.

Improvements to property rented by a person with a disability

Amounts paid to buy and install special plumbing fixtures for a person with a disability (mainly for medical reasons) in a rented house are medical expenses.

Example: Improvements installed by a disabled tenant

Javier has arthritis and a heart condition. He can't climb stairs or get into a bathtub. On his doctor's advice, he installs a bathroom with a shower stall on the first floor of his two-story rented house.

The landlord didn't pay any of the cost of buying and installing the special plumbing and didn't lower the rent. Javier can include the entire amount he paid as a qualified medical expense.

Car

The cost of special hand controls and other special equipment installed in a car for the use of a person with a disability.

Car, special design

Difference between the cost of a regular car and a car designed to hold a wheelchair.

Car, transportation expenses

Out-of-pocket expenses, such as the cost of gas and oil, when a car is used for medical reasons are eligible. Depreciation, insurance, general repair, and maintenance expenses are not.

In lieu of actual expenses, a standard mileage rate for use of a car for medical reasons is eligible. To find the current mileage rate for medical treatment, go to www.irs.gov. Parking fees and tolls are eligible whether actual expenses or the standard mileage rate are used.

Chiropractor

Christian Science practitioner

Contact lenses

Needed for medical reasons (such as correcting vision or protecting the eye); cost of equipment and materials required for using contact lenses, such as saline solution and enzyme cleaner. See Eyeglasses and eye surgery.

Cosmetic surgery (reconstructive)

If necessary to improve a deformity arising from, or directly related to, a congenital abnormality, a personal injury resulting from an accident or trauma, or a disfiguring disease.

Crutches

Purchase or rental.

Dental treatment

Includes fees paid to dentists for X-rays, fillings, braces, extractions, dentures, etc.

Diagnostic devices

For diagnosing and treating illness and disease, such as diabetic testing equipment and supplies.

Disabled dependent care expenses

Some may qualify as either medical expenses or work-related expenses for purposes of taking a credit for dependent care. This can be applied either way as long as you don't use the same expenses to claim both a credit and a medical expense deduction.

Drug addiction

Inpatient treatment at a drug treatment center, including meals and lodging.

Drugs

See medicines.

Eyeglasses

Needed for medical reasons; can also include fees paid for eye examinations.

Eye surgery

To treat illnesses, injuries, and defective vision (laser eye surgery or radial keratotomy).

Fertility enhancement

Procedures such as in vitro fertilization (including temporary storage of eggs or sperm) or surgery, including an operation to reverse prior surgery that prevented fertility.

Founder's fee

See lifetime care—advance payments.

Guide dog or other service animal

To be used by a visually impaired or hearing-impaired person; the cost of a dog or other service animal trained to assist persons with other physical disabilities; amounts paid for the ongoing care of service animals.

Health institute

Only if prescribed by a physician and the physician issues a statement that the treatment is necessary to alleviate a physical or mental defect or illness of the individual receiving the treatment.

Health maintenance organization (HMO)

Premiums paid for yourself, your spouse, or a dependent to receive medical care from a health maintenance organization. See insurance premiums.

Hearing aids

Including batteries to operate hearing aids.

Home care

See nursing services.

Home improvements

See capital expenses.

Hospital services

Cost of inpatient care at a hospital or similar institution if the principal reason for being there is to receive medical care; includes amounts paid for meals and lodging. Also see lodging.

Insurance premiums

HSA funds can be used to pay for insurance premiums under the following circumstances:

- You are collecting federal or state unemployment benefits.

- You have COBRA continuation coverage through a former employer.

- You have a qualified long-term care insurance contract (subject to additional limitations).

If you have a policy that provides more than one kind of payment, you can include the premiums for the medical care part of the policy if the charge for the medical part is reasonable. The cost of the medical part must be separately stated in the insurance contract or given to you in a separate statement.

Note: If advance payments of the health coverage tax credit are made on an individual's behalf to an insurance company, don't include any advance payments made when figuring the amount the individual may deduct for insurance premiums. Also, if this individual is claiming the health coverage tax credit, the individual can subtract the amount shown on line 4 of Form 8885 (reduced by any advance payments shown on line 6) from the total insurance premiums paid.

- Medicare Part A premiums. If covered under Social Security (or if a government employee who paid Medicare tax), an individual is enrolled in Medicare A. The payroll tax paid for Medicare A is not a medical expense.

If the individual isn't covered by Social Security (or wasn't a government employee who paid Medicare tax), he/she can voluntarily enroll in Medicare A. In this situation, the premiums the individual pays for Medicare A can be included as a medical expense on her tax return.

- Medicare Part B premiums. Medicare B is a supplemental medical insurance plan. Premiums paid for Medicare B are a medical expense.

  If an individual applied for Medicare B at 65 or after he became disabled, he or she can deduct the monthly premiums paid. If you were over 65 or disabled when you first enrolled, check the information you received from the Social Security Administration to find out your premium.

- Medicare Part C (Medicare Advantage) premiums.

- Medicare Part D premiums.

- Prepaid insurance premiums. Premiums paid before 65 for insurance for medical care for an individual, a spouse, or dependents after an individual reaches 65 are medical care expenses in the year paid if:

  - Payable in equal yearly installments or more often

  - Payable for at least 10 years, or until the individual reaches age 65 (but not for less than five years)

Laboratory fees

If part of medical care.

Lead-based paint removal

The cost of removing lead-based paints from surfaces in the home to prevent a child who has or had lead poisoning from eating the paint.

The surfaces must be in poor repair (peeling or cracking) or within the child's reach. The cost of repainting the scraped area isn't a medical expense.

If, instead of removing the paint, the area is covered with wallboard or paneling, treat these items as capital expenses. See capital expenses. The cost of painting the wallboard can't be included as a medical expense.

Learning disability

See special education.

Legal fees

To authorize treatment for mental illness.

Lifetime care—advance payments

Part of a life-care fee or founder's fee paid monthly or as a lump sum under an agreement with a retirement home.

The part of the payment included is the amount properly allocable to medical care. The agreement must require that an individual pay a specific fee as a condition for the home's promise to provide lifetime care that includes medical care.

An individual can use a statement from the retirement home to prove the amount properly allocable to medical care. The statement must be based either on the home's prior experience or on information from a comparable home.

- Dependents with disabilities. Advance payments to a private institution for lifetime care, treatment, and training a physically or mentally impaired child upon the caregiver's death or when the caregiver becomes unable to provide care. The payments must be a condition for the institution's future acceptance of the child and must not be refundable.

- Payments for future medical care. Generally, an individual can't include in medical expenses current payments for medical care (including medical insurance) to be provided substantially beyond the end of the year. This rule doesn't apply in situations where the future care is purchased in connection with obtaining lifetime care of the type described above (see dependents with disabilities).

Lodging

Cost of meals and lodging at a hospital or similar institution if a principal reason for being there is to receive medical care. See nursing home.

An individual may be able to include in medical expenses the cost of lodging not provided in a hospital or similar institution. The individual can include the cost of such lodging while away from home if all of the following requirements are met:

- The lodging is primarily for and essential to medical care.

- The medical care is provided by a doctor in a licensed hospital or in a medical care facility related to, or the equivalent of, a licensed hospital.

- The lodging isn't lavish or extravagant under the circumstances.

- There is no significant element of personal pleasure, recreation, or vacation in the travel away from home.

The amount included in medical expenses for lodging can't be more than $50 for each night for each person. The individual can include lodging for a person traveling with the person receiving the medical care. For example, if a parent is traveling with a sick child, up to $100 per night can be included as a medical expense for lodging. Meals aren't included.

Don't include the cost of lodging while away from home for medical treatment if that treatment isn't received from a doctor in a licensed hospital or in a medical care facility related to, or the equivalent of, a licensed hospital or if that lodging isn't primarily for or essential to the medical care received.

Long-term care

Amounts paid for qualified long-term care services and premiums paid for qualified long-term care insurance contracts.

Long-term qualified care services

Necessary diagnostic, preventive, therapeutic, curing, treating, mitigating, rehabilitative services, and maintenance and personal care services (defined below) that are:

- Required by a chronically ill individual

- Provided as the result of a plan of care prescribed by a licensed healthcare practitioner.

- An individual is chronically ill if, within the previous 12 months, a licensed healthcare practitioner has certified that the individual meets either of the following descriptions:

  - He or she is unable to perform at least two activities of daily living without substantial assistance from another individual for at least 90 days, due to a loss of functional capacity. Activities of daily living are eating, using the restroom, transferring, bathing, dressing, and continence.

  - He or she requires substantial supervision to be protected from threats to health and safety due to severe cognitive impairment.

- Maintenance and personal care services. Care that has as its primary purpose providing a chronically ill individual with needed assistance with their disabilities (including protection from threats to health and safety due to severe cognitive impairment).

Long-term qualified care insurance contracts

An insurance contract that provides only coverage of qualified long-term care services.

The contract must:

- Be guaranteed renewable.

- Not provide for a cash surrender value or other money that can be paid, assigned, pledged, or borrowed.

- Provide that refunds, other than refunds on the death of the insured or complete surrender or cancellation of the contract, and dividends under the contract must be used only to reduce future premiums or increase future benefits.

- Not pay or reimburse expenses incurred for services or items that would be reimbursed under Medicare, except where Medicare is a secondary payer.

- Qualified long-term care premiums. Qualified long-term care premiums, up to the amounts shown below, can be included as medical expenses on Schedule A (Form 1040). The limit on premiums is for each person as of 2018:

  - Age 40 or under: $420

  - Age 41 to 50: $780

- Age 51 to 60: $1,560

- Age 61 to 70: $4,160

- Age 71 or over: $5,200

- Unreimbursed expenses for qualified long-term care services.

Meals

The cost of meals at a hospital or similar institution if a principal reason for being there is to get medical care. The cost of meals that aren't part of inpatient care are ineligible.

Medical conferences

Amounts paid for admission and transportation to a medical conference if the medical conference concerns the chronic illness of an individual, a spouse, or a dependent.

The costs of the medical conference must be primarily for and necessary to the medical care of an individual, a spouse, or a dependent. The majority of the time spent at the conference must be spent attending sessions on medical information.

The cost of meals and lodging while attending the conference is not deductible as a medical expense.

Medical information plan

Amounts paid to a plan that keeps medical information in a computer data bank and retrieves and furnishes the information on request to an attending physician.

Medical services

Amounts paid for legal or medical services provided by:

- Physicians

- Surgeons

- Specialists

- Other medical practitioners

Medicare Part A

Covers hospital insurance that pays for inpatient hospital stays, care in a skilled nursing facility, hospice care, and some home healthcare.

Medicare Part B

A form medical insurance that helps pay for doctors' services, outpatient hospital care, durable medical equipment, and some medical services that aren't covered by Part A.

Medicines

Medications prescribed by a provider to treat a specific medical condition.

In response to the COVID-19 pandemic, Congress passed the Coronavirus Aid, Relief, and Economic Security (CARES) Act. Included in the Act was a provision to allow HSA owners to use HSA funds to purchase over-the-counter drugs and medication without needing a prescription. The provision is retroactive to January 1, 2020.

Menstrual care products

The CARES Act added menstrual care products as a qualified medical expense. Applicable products include tampons, pads, liners, cups, sponges, or similar products. Feminine hygiene products are not considered a qualified medical expense.

Mentally challenged, special homes for

Costs of keeping a mentally challenged person in a special home, not the home of a relative, on the recommendation of a psychiatrist to help the person adjust from life in a mental hospital to community living.

Nursing home

Costs of medical care for an individual, a spouse or a dependent in a nursing home, home for the aged or similar institution, including the cost of meals and lodging in the home if a principal reason is to get medical care.

If the reason for being in the home is personal, the cost of meals and lodging is ineligible.

Nursing services

Wages and other amounts paid for nursing services.

Services need not be performed by a nurse as long as the services are of a kind generally performed by a nurse. This includes services connected with caring for a patient's condition, such as giving medication or changing dressings, as well as bathing and grooming the patient. Services can be provided at home or in a care facility.

Generally, only the amount spent for nursing services is a medical expense. If the attendant also provides personal and household services, amounts paid to the attendant must be divided between the time spent performing household and personal services and the time spent for nursing services. However, certain maintenance or personal care services provided for qualified long-term care can be included as medical expenses. Additionally, certain expenses for household services or for the care of a qualifying individual incurred to allow you to work may qualify for the child and dependent care credit (See IRS Publication 503—Child and Dependent Care Expenses).

Part of the amount paid for that attendant's meals is also eligible. Divide the food expense among the household members to find the cost of the attendant's food. Then divide that cost in the same manner as in the preceding paragraph. If additional amounts were paid for household upkeep because of the attendant, these amounts can be included. This includes extra rent or utilities paid because of a move to a larger apartment to provide space for the attendant.

- Employment taxes. Social Security tax, FUTA, Medicare tax, and state employment taxes paid for a nurse, attendant, or other person who provides medical care[1].

- If the attendant also provides personal and household services, the amount of employment taxes paid for medical services as explained under nursing services is eligible.

Operations

Amounts paid for legal operations that aren't for unnecessary unprescribed cosmetic surgery.

Optometrist

See eyeglasses.

---

1 See IRS Publication 926—Household Employer's Tax Guide

Organ donors

See transplants.

Osteopath

Oxygen

Oxygen equipment to relieve breathing problems caused by a medical condition.

Prosthesis

See artificial limb.

Psychiatric care

Includes the cost of supporting a mentally ill dependent at a specially equipped medical center where the dependent receives medical care.

See psychoanalysis and transportation.

Psychoanalysis

Psychologist

Amounts paid for medical care.

Special education

Fees paid on a doctor's recommendation for a child's tutoring by a teacher who is specially trained and qualified to work with children with learning disabilities caused by mental or physical impairments, including nervous system disorders.

An individual can include as medical expenses the cost (tuition, meals, and lodging) of attending a school that furnishes special education to help a child overcome learning disabilities. A doctor must recommend that the child attend the school.

- Overcoming learning disabilities must be a principal reason for attending the school, and any ordinary education received must be incidental to the special education provided. Special education includes:

- Teaching braille to a visually impaired person

- Teaching lip reading to a hearing-impaired person

- Giving remedial language training to correct a condition caused by a birth defect

An individual can't include in medical expenses the cost of sending a child to a school where the course of study and the disciplinary methods have a beneficial effect on the child's attitude if the availability of medical care in the school isn't a principal reason for sending the student there.

Sterilization

Legally performed operation to make a person unable to have children.

Stop-smoking programs

Note that amounts paid for drugs that do not require a prescription, such as nicotine gum or patches, designed to help stop smoking are ineligible.

Surgery

See operations.

Telephone

Cost of special telephone equipment that lets a hearing-impaired person communicate over a regular telephone and the cost of repairing the equipment.

Television

Equipment that displays the audio part of television programs as subtitles for hearing-impaired persons; may be the cost of an adapter that attaches to a regular set or part of the cost of a specially equipped television that exceeds the cost of the same model regular television set.

Therapy

Received as medical treatment.

Patterning exercises

For a mentally challenged child—must consist mainly of coordinated physical manipulation of the child's arms and legs to imitate crawling and other normal movements.

Transplants

Medical care received because an individual is a donor or possible donor of a kidney or other organ; and medical care of a donor in connection with the donating of an organ to another individual, including transportation. Transportation includes the following guidelines:

- Transportation primarily for, and essential to, medical care—including bus, taxi, train or plane fares, or ambulance services

- Transportation expenses of a parent who must go with a child who needs medical care

- Transportation expenses of a nurse or other person who can give injections, medications, or other treatment required by a patient who is traveling to get medical care and can't travel alone

- Transportation expenses for regular visits to see a mentally ill dependent, if these visits are recommended as a part of treatment

Transportation

You can include in medical expenses amounts paid for transportation primarily for, and essential to, medical care.

- Bus, taxi, train or plane fares, or ambulance service

- Transportation expenses of a parent who must go with a child who needs medical care

- Transportation expenses of a nurse or other person who can give injections, medications, or other treatment required by a patient who is traveling to get medical care and is unable to travel alone

- Transportation expenses for regular visits to see a mentally ill dependent, if these visits are recommended as a part of treatment

Trips

Transportation to another city if the trip is primarily for, and essential to, receiving medical services are eligible. See lodging and medical conferences.

Tuition

Under special circumstances, charges for tuition are eligible. See special education. Charges for a health plan included in a lump sum tuition fee are eligible if the charges are stated separately or can easily be obtained from the school.

Vasectomy

A surgery performed to affect sterility in men.

Veterinary fees

Care of guide dogs for the seeing-impaired or hearing-impaired and other service animals specially trained to assist persons with physical disabilities are eligible.

Vision correction surgery

See eye surgery.

Weight-loss program

Amounts paid to lose weight if it is a treatment for a specific disease diagnosed by a physician, such as obesity, hypertension, or heart disease, are eligible, including fees paid for membership in a weight-reduction group and attendance at periodic meetings.

The cost of special food is eligible only if:

- The food doesn't satisfy normal nutritional needs.

- The food alleviates or treats an illness.

- The need for the food is substantiated by a physician.

- The amount included as medical expenses is limited to the amount by which the cost of the special food exceeds the cost of a normal diet.

Wheelchair

Amounts paid to rent, purchase, operate, and maintain an autoette or wheelchair used mainly for the relief of sickness or disability and not just to provide transportation to and from work.

Wig

Cost of a wig purchased on the advice of a physician for the mental health of a patient who has lost all of his or her hair from disease or treatment.

X-ray

For medical reasons.

APPENDIX D

Ineligible medical and dental expenses

The following items cannot be used when calculating a medical expense deduction.

Babysitting

Amounts paid for the care of normal healthy babies and children, even if the expenses enable an individual, a spouse, or a dependent to get medical or dental treatment are ineligible. Any expense allowed as a childcare credit can't be treated as an expense paid for medical care.

Controlled substances

Such as marijuana, laetrile, etc., in violation of federal law.

Cosmetic surgery

Including any procedure directed at improving the patient's appearance that doesn't meaningfully promote the proper function of the body or prevent or treat illness or disease, such as face lifts, hair transplants, hair removal (electrolysis), tooth whitening, and liposuction.

Dancing lessons

As well as swimming lessons and other lessons, even if recommended by a doctor for the improvement of general health.

Diaper service

Diapers or diaper services, unless needed to relieve the effects of a particular disease.

Electrolysis or hair removal

See cosmetic surgery.

Employer-sponsored health insurance plan

Any insurance premiums paid by an employer-sponsored health insurance plan unless the premiums are included in box 1 of Form W-2; any other medical and dental expenses paid by the plan unless the amount paid is included in box 1 of Form W-2.

Example Premiums paid with pre-tax dollars

You are a federal employee participating in the Federal Employee Health Benefits (FEHB) program.

Your share of the FEHB premium is paid with pretax dollars. Because you're an employee whose insurance premiums are paid with money that's never included in your gross income, you can't deduct the premiums paid with that money.

Funeral expenses

Funeral expenses may be deductible on the decedent's federal estate tax return.

Future medical care

Care to be provided substantially beyond the end of the year is ineligible. This doesn't apply to situations where the future care is purchased in connection with obtaining lifetime care of the type described under long-term care.

Hair transplant

See cosmetic surgery.

Health club dues

Or amounts paid to improve one's general health or to relieve physical or mental discomfort not related to a particular medical condition; the cost of membership in any club organized for business, pleasure, recreation, or other social purpose.

Health coverage tax credit

Household help

Even if such help is recommended by a doctor, this is a personal expense that isn't deductible. However, certain expenses paid to a person providing nursing-type services may be eligible. For more information, see nursing services. Also, certain maintenance or personal care services provided for qualified long-term care is eligible. For more information, see qualified long-term care services.

Illegal operations and treatments

Or controlled substances whether rendered or prescribed by licensed or unlicensed practitioners.

Insurance premiums

- Life insurance policies

- Policies providing payment for loss of earnings

- Policies for loss of life, limb, sight, etc.

- Policies that pay a guaranteed amount each week for a stated number of weeks if hospitalized for sickness or injury

- The part of car insurance premiums that provides medical insurance coverage for all persons injured in or by a car because the part of the premium for an individual, a spouse, or a dependent isn't stated separately from the part of the premium for medical care for others

- Medicare Medigap premiums

Legal fees

Management of a guardianship estate, fees for conducting the affairs of the person being treated, or other fees that aren't necessary for medical care.

Maternity clothes

Medical Savings Account (MSA)

Or medical expenses paid for with a tax-free distribution from an Archer MSA or other funds equal to the amount of the distribution. For more information on Archer MSAs, see IRS Publication 969—Medical Savings Accounts (MSAs).

Nutritional supplements

Vitamins, herbal supplements, natural medicines, etc., unless recommended by a medical practitioner as treatment for a specific medical condition diagnosed by a physician.

Personal use items

The cost of an item ordinarily used for personal, living, or family purposes, unless used primarily to prevent or alleviate a physical or mental defect or illness.

For example, the cost of a toothbrush and toothpaste is a nondeductible personal expense.

An item purchased in a special form primarily to alleviate a physical defect is one that in normal form is ordinarily used for personal, living, or family purposes, the excess of the cost of the special form over the cost of the normal form is a medical expense. See braille books and magazines.

Sick leave (unused sick leave used to pay premiums)

An individual can include in gross income cash payments received at the time of retirement for unused sick leave. An individual can also include in gross income the value of unused sick leave that, at the individual's option, the employer applies to the cost of continuing participation in the employer's health plan after the individual retires. The cost of continuing participation in the health plan is eligible.

If an individual participates in a health plan where the employer automatically applies the value of unused sick leave to the cost of continuing participation in the health plan (and the individual doesn't have the option to receive cash), the individual can't include the value of the unused sick leave in gross income. The individual can't include this cost of continuing participation in that health plan as a medical expense.

Swimming lessons

See dancing lessons.

Teeth whitening

See cosmetic surgery.

Transportation expenses

- Going to and from work, even if the condition requires an unusual means of transportation

- Travel to another city for an operation or other medical care

- Travel that is merely for the general improvement of health

- Weight-loss program.
When for the improvement of appearance, general health, or sense of well-being, including amounts paid to lose weight unless the weight loss is a treatment for a specific disease diagnosed by a physician (such as obesity, hypertension, or heart disease). Includes fees paid for membership in a weight-reduction group and attendance at periodic meetings. Also, membership dues for a gym, health club, or spa; the cost of diet food or beverages because the diet food and beverages substitute for what is normally consumed to satisfy nutritional needs; the cost of special food unless all three of the following requirements are met:

  - The food does not satisfy normal nutritional needs.

  - The food alleviates or treats an illness.

  - The need for the food is substantiated by a physician.

The eligible amount is limited to the amount by which the cost of the special food exceeds the cost of a normal diet.